Street Journal
Finding God in the Homeless

Selections from the notebooks of
Gary N. Smith, S.J.

Sheed & Ward

Sheed & Ward™ is a service of The National Catholic Reporter Publishing Company.

Library of Congress Cataloguing in Publication Data

Smith, Gary N., 1937-
    Street journal : finding God in the homeless : selections from the notebooks of Gary N. Smith, S.J.
       p.   cm.
    Includes bibliographical references.
    ISBN 1-55612-656-5 (alk. paper)
    1. Smith, Gary N., 1937-   . 2. Catholic Church--Washington (State)--Tacoma--Clergy--Diaries. 3. Nativity House (Tacoma, Wash.) 4. Church work with the homeless--Washington (State)--Tacoma. 5. Church work with the poor--Washington (State)--Tacoma. 6. Church work with the poor--Catholic Church. 7. Tacoma (Wash.)--Church history. I. Title.
BX4705.S66254A3   1994
282'.092--dc20
[B]   93-29463
                                                                 CIP

Published by: Sheed & Ward
              115 E. Armour Blvd.
              P.O. Box 419492
              Kansas City, MO 64141

To order, call: (800) 333-7373

Cover design copyright© 1994 by Mark McIntyre, S.J.

Contents

Acknowledgments

Bernanos, Georges, *The Diary of a Country Priest* (New York: The Macmillan Company, 1969), p. 255.

Carver, Raymond, from the poem, "Proposal," in *A New Path to the Waterfall* (New York: Atlantic Monthly Press, 1990), p. 115.

Hesse, Herman, *Narcissus and Goldmund* (New York: Bantam Books, 1968), p. 306.

Hopkins, Gerard Manley, from the poem "God's Grandeur," in *Gerard Manley Hopkins* (London: Penguin Classics, 1953), p. 2.

Kierkegaard, Soren, *The Prayers of Soren Kierkegaard*, edited by Perry LeFerve, (Chicago: University of Chicago Press, 1963).

Merton, Thomas, from the letter to Jim Forest in *Hidden Ground of Love, Letters of Thomas Merton*, Edited by William H. Shannon (New York: Farrar, Straus, Giroux, 1985) pp. 294-297.

Miller, Arthur, from the play, *After the Fall* (New York: Viking Press, 1964), p. 24.

Moody, John, *John Henry Newman* (New York: Sheed & Ward, 1945) p. 34.

All scriptural excerpts are from *The Jerusalem Bible* (Garden City, New York: Doubleday & Company, 1966).

To the people of the streets who loved and taught me,
To Jeri who always believed in me,
To the Staff and Board of Directors of Nativity House
  who shared the vision with me,
To my brother Jesuits who have inspired me,
To Lynn who encouraged and helped me to write this,
In deep and lasting gratitude.

❖ *Introduction* ❖

Moving past the empty storefronts and warehouses along the old sidewalks of South Commerce Street in downtown Tacoma, Washington, one eventually arrives at Nativity House. It is a daytime drop-in center for the people of the streets. It opened on Christmas Eve of 1979 and, since then, has been a place of food, clothing, and warmth.

I came to Nativity House in the summer of 1984. I had just concluded eight years in Oakland, California, where I worked with a team of Jesuit community organizers, their collaborators, and neighborhood activists. The growing homeless problem in the United States, which emerged in the early eighties, led me to taking the position of Director of Nativity House.

It is not a large center, but approximately 200 persons pass through each day, using its restroom, clothesroom, and telephone. They share in its two daily meals, and some participate in the two weekly Catholic Masses that are offered. For all, this small building is a refuge from the wilderness and alienation of the streets.

Nativity House operates on the donations of many good people and is fueled by the spirit of its staff, volunteers, and Board of Directors. Its fundamental mission is one of imitation of Jesus who described his vocation in the words of the prophet Isaiah:

> He has sent me to bring the good news to the poor;
> to bind up hearts that are broken;
> to proclaim liberty to the captives;
> to comfort all those who mourn. (Is. 61: 1-2)

The commanding and consoling truth in Matthew's Gospel is the heart of Nativity House: Jesus identified himself with the poor.

> Then the virtuous will say to him in reply, "Lord, when did we see you hungry and feed you; or thirsty and give you drink? When did we see you a stranger and make you welcome; naked and clothe you; sick or in prison and go to see you?" And the King will answer, "I tell you solemnly, in so far as you did this to one of the least of these

brothers and sisters of mine, you did it to me." (Mt. 25:37-41)

To walk into Nativity House is to enter the world of the poor and the hidden. They are our guests. Sitting or standing, silent or chatting, they are a remarkable mix of human beings. Our guests are of all ages, all races, and approximately eighty percent of them are men. They include the temporarily and chronically unemployed, homeless couples with their children, burned-out Vietnam Veterans, drug addicts, female and male prostitutes, chronic alcoholics, itinerant farm workers, hoboes, bag ladies, the mentally ill, undocumented aliens, pimps, the developmentally disabled, ex-convicts, thugs, disaffected teenagers, and lonely seniors.

Almost all are homeless, which is to say that they either have no permanent address or live in a temporary residence. Most live and sleep in shelters, cheap hotels and apartments, cars, fields, or on sidewalks.

While I was Director, I wrote in a notebook of some of my day-to-day experiences from mid-1984 to the autumn of 1991. Some episodes, personal encounters, and reflections are presented here. For the most part, I have changed names in order to preserve the anonymity of guests.

My purpose in writing this book is two-fold. First, I want to share with the reader the personal and human side of the homeless street people of America. It is a side which is vague and faceless and insignificant in our culture. Secondly, my purpose is to convey the story of my own growth and transformation as I participated in the lives of our guests; as a human being and as a Jesuit priest, my life was changed. Within the scope of this latter purpose, I am not so much sharing my journal as I am telling a love story.

Street Journal

❖ *1984* ❖

Damn Prosthesis

Thursday, June 28th

It has begun, this entry into the streets of Tacoma. I am exhausted, after one day. The demands on every one of my senses and my skills and plain old street savvy can be enormous. There are power surges in me all day as I move among so many broken and strange people: seniors and teenagers; addicts and chronic alcoholics; extroverts and the withdrawn; the sane and insane; the friendly; the bitter; the tough; the gentle.

Already I have touched some awful things, like seeing young men and women lining up at the Tacoma Plasma Center to sell their blood for busfare and who-knows-what. Businesses are making bucks off the blood of the poor; what a grim metaphor for all those enterprises which connect the exploited with the exploiters.

Somewhere I had a discussion with an old man, reeking of the smell of dried urine. He refused to give me his name, but was extravagant in his stories of living off his wits and garbage dumpsters ("MacDonald's throws out some great burgers after they close."). One middle-aged woman, Ann, wearing at least three heavy coats, was effusive as she welcomed me and shared with me in a hushed voice all the latest street gossip. A sullen young man looked up from his novel as I tried to introduce myself. He said, "Fuck you," and moved to another chair.

What am I getting into here? How does God fit in? God fits in—of course—but in the midst of so many lost faces, it would take the tortured reasoning of a theologian to make the connections between Creator and creature. Maybe I'm the theologian. Maybe I am one of the connections.

Sunday, July 1st

She simply sat there, coffee cup in hand. Everything about her face was frozen in grief, an inside-out sorrow. Even her tears seemed to move slowly. Holly was her name, 22 years old, in her fourth pregnancy. Her other three children were apparently stashed away with relatives who have kissed her off because of

3

her out-of-control drinking. Any and all relationships with men
have crashed and burned.

It was a nervous conversation for both of us; me, the rookie
Director of Nativity House, trying to communicate and act like I
was cool and knew the score; she, wanting badly to trust, but
fearing that trust—or what appeared to be trust—was just an experience of self-delusion. And I was another man, that quick-
sand of her life. There must have been many terrible and unspeakable nights and days in this woman's life.

I went to get coffee refills. She left while I was gone.

Is this what it is going to be like: a quick, super-charged
investment of concern and care on my part, and then the whole
thing returned as empty as the table and chairs where Holly and
I were talking? Yet, I need to remind myself that it is a fearful
experience to share oneself. It is a big risk when the past consequences of such sharing have been hurt and betrayal.

Tuesday, July 10th

The days begin to roll by; at the end of each one, I am
wired with the ebb and flow of many people. The paradox of
the streets—or one of them—is that there can be so much grind-
ing boredom, and yet the time races by.

Today was a test in the art of crisis management. Max, a
rock-solid drifter got into a pushing match with Ray, a loud-
mouthed, set-em-up-bartender, World War II veteran. Even as I
separated them, they continued to exchange verbal shots over
my shoulder. Then, to my horror, Max grabbed a butcher knife,
which we had carelessly left on the kitchen counter (Lesson # 1),
and postured menacingly. Nativity House guests became silent,
waiting. In a rush of adrenalin, I shouted in Max's face, ordering
him to give me the bleeping knife. He handed it over meekly.
But machismo Ray had not finished. Standing ten feet away
from Max and me, using language that should have burned the
paint off the wall, he proceeded to unstrap his leg and throw it at
Max. The artifical leg (the real one was blown off in the South
Pacific) whirled past our ducked heads, and, as I was going

down, I thought of one of those Australian boomerangs, wondering if the damn prosthesis would make a turn at the door and return to carry out its owner's vengeance, who was now hopping around on one leg, swearing steadily. "This is great," I thought, "decapitated by a flying leg in my first month on the job."

In the end, with the help of Beth and Kevin, two of my staff people, we talked some sense into Max and Ray. They left arm and arm, all appendages safely attached.

Wednesday, July 18th

My preoccupation tonight is with the transitory nature of friendship on the streets. Already I have met and befriended some extraordinary people; they are individuals of ruthless honesty, possess an ability to express their care, and have an unspoken, but obvious kind of loyalty toward me. Yet tomorrow they may be gone, drifting on to the next stop, the next moment, fading into the murky nooks and crannies of this city or of this country.

I have developed a genuine care for Too-Tall Raul, the giant hobo, and he for me. I took him—crammed into my little Toyota—to the Tacoma Detox Center on Sunday. He returned on Wednesday, drunk out of his skull. The big guy longs for meaning and purpose in his life, but has not a clue on how to unravel his pain. He is a child of rejection ("My daddy told me I was a mistake and a fun night in the sack"), a Thunderbird wine alcoholic, and a veteran of twenty-six years of lonely riding on the rails. He is full of defenses and the convoluted thinking that invades the soul when we walk alone with no end in sight. But as he stood there this morning, all six foot, ten inches of him, a filthy Oregon State baseball cap perched on this big shock of hair, and grinning toothlessly at me, I thought of how his goodness has not been sucked out of him in spite of it all. He looked down on me (I am tall and still seven inches smaller) and announced that he was heading for Astoria. And so, huge backpack strapped in place, he left town.

This is a work of faith. It is the faith which believes that a solitary touch in the night might move a person toward wholeness, toward some elementary sense of his or her own dignity, in a world which creates many obstacles to the realization of that dignity. It is a ministry of presence, and we have to make those acts of love which proceed from that faith. I remember Pat and Dick, a young couple I knew in a parish in San Jose, who had a severely retarded son, Sean. They used to pump classical music into his room on those occasions when he was not being held in their arms.

I asked them once why they did this. They responded, "You never know what is getting through." Isn't that a truth that drives our love here on the streets, the belief that something is reaching the heart, no matter how minuscule and homely the gift of care and presence may be? I think of the character in Bernanos' *Diary of a Country Priest* who said, "Grace is everywhere."

Wednesday, August 8th

People use many resources to survive. It is really disgusting to see the thriving business of the selling and buying of plasma on the streets. People here talk about where they can get the most money for their blood with the intensity of Wall Street brokers analyzing companies and numbers. Those with low iron counts figure out how to feed their emaciated blood like the marathon runners who load their blood systems with lots of carbohydrates.

There is an army of individuals who are professional dumpster divers, moving out every day with their plastic bags, human scavengers sifting the garbage for aluminum cans or any of the valuables of a throw-away America: radios, clothes, clocks, furniture, shoes, car parts, a million knickknacks. And food. My God, the food. One old pro brought in a huge bag of "fresh" day-old sandwiches, discovered in a dumpster behind a local deli. "Can you use them, Father?"

From food to recyclables to drugs, the streets have an infinite number of cottage industries.

Thursday, August 23rd

I met this extraordinary fellow, Phil, recently. He is an old-looking fifty, mentally ill, but functional. He sits quietly in a corner or paces up and down Nativity House. He is always dressed in rumpled clothing, his hair hanging down over his grimaced face. Phil resides in that bat cave, the Majestic Hotel, apparently living on a small disability check. His brother, a physician in Los Angeles, is the payee, who also doles out some weekly spending money. Phil is a former math major from the University of Utah who simply lost it along the way and now spends most of his thinking time in that strange world of the compulsive personality. His compulsion is numbers. At different times he will talk to me, starting out slowly, hesitatingly, then get into a roll and center most of his thoughts around the mathematical implications of the Old Testament. Yesterday, he shifted into his theory of numbers and music, especially as they are applied to the techniques of playing the piano. Sensing an opportunity to crack through to something more personable, I commented that I would like to hear him play the piano sometime. He stopped dead in his theoretical tracks, studied me, and asked if I would really like to hear him play. Sure, I said. He left immediately, telling me with a parting shot that he would go and get his piano. He returned with one of those $19.95 beauties which he probably purchased at the local Woolworth's.

In the confines of our tiny office (room for a tiny desk, a tiny chair, and two tiny people), this guy played—for me—the concert of the century. His repertoire consisted only of three and a half songs because in the world of Phil's number theories anything beyond three and a half songs led to some kind of immanent destruction. His songs were "Three Blind Mice," "Silent Night," "O Come All Ye Faithful," and one half of "Twinkle, Twinkle Little Star." Of course, throughout his presentation Phil would point out, with all the seriousness and insight of a college instructor, how he applied his musical number theories. I had this feeling, a couple of times, that he was pleased to explain certain chord structures that I obviously did not know.

After the concert, he rambled on into yet another version of the relationship between numbers and the Book of Genesis. Later, after lunch, Phil wandered out the door, walking down Commerce Street with his piano under his arm.

Sunday, September 9th

Every Sunday morning, after a big 9 AM breakfast, we have Mass.

A small, knee-high altar is placed in the back of the large room which makes up the bulk of Nativity House. As I look out from behind the altar, I am surrounded by my congregation. They are seated in our old couches and beat-up chairs or standing against the walls. There are many of our guests who prefer not to participate in the service, but remain in the back where they read or sleep or listen. I always ask someone to read a scripture passage, and, at some point, in English and Spanish, all offer their own special intentions for which they want to pray. The prayers are touching: for family scattered throughout the world; for the courage to overcome substance abuse; for employment; for acquaintances in jail; for a safe trip home; for the volunteers who have prepared the hot breakfast; for dead comrades; for the needs of friends. At communion time, all are invited to share in the broken bread and the chalice of wine.

It is not a fancy liturgy, but rich in genuine and open piety. We tell our story of God in our life and share in a Eucharistic meal. I am consoled to be involved in this part of the lives of our guests. I claim my life as a priest more honestly—going to the heart of the matter—when I am a bread-breaker in this community and when I facilitate the story telling of faith in the lean and spare surroundings of skid row.

At Mass today, as I was distributing communion, Francis, behind me, was calming down Phil whose mathematics could not handle the Gospel passage about Jesus and the ten lepers.

Shaking his head, becoming more and more agitated, Phil was
working himself into a psychic meltdown. Francis was holding
Phil's hand and carefully talking him down. A cathedral would
weep to have this kind of wisdom and compassion present.

Tuesday, September 15th

A Vietnam Veteran known as Scarface Al, wept in my office
today. He is a huge guy, two Silver Stars, a couple of Purple
Hearts, and plates in his head. He was utterly lost and broken,
and, as he clung to me, I felt the fury giving way, momentarily,
to the longing to belong—to someone, something, somewhere,
somehow.

At such moments, I am aware of my own lack of sanctity in
the presence of such holiness, wondering how on earth I can be
an instrument of God's grace, some kind of island of meaning in
the ocean of chaos. One always feels so poor with the mentally
ill or the Vietnam Vet. Maybe I have it all wrong: these moments
are for me as much as for them. We need each other when we
suffer and when we are lost. Al is teaching me how to be compassionate and how to reach out in my own suffering.

Thursday, October 18th

In the middle of breakfast this morning, Dan, a very-to-him-
self Sioux, eerily stood up, bowl of cereal tumbling to the floor.
He held an imaginary rifle in his hands. At that moment, he was
in a Cambodian rice paddy, calling out to his cousin up ahead,
waiting for an answer that would never come. As suddenly as
Dan was out of it, he came into it, turned to me and shouted,
"How can a compassionate God allow so many to die in Vietnam?" I tried to answer. It was, to that point in my life, the
ultimate theological discussion, the showdown between raw life
and religious buzzwords. It was no contest. My words sounded

so empty, so disconnected from the pain I saw on that man's face.

Dan and I talked again, later in the day, both winding up in tears. He cried over the loss of a gunned-down brother who came back in an army plastic bag ("His face was blown off") and a cousin who never came back. I cried because I couldn't do anything else, but cry. I am learning here that silent respect for grief means more than some sort of expressed clerical insight. Be silent, be still, before the mystery of it all. So, with Dan, it became a matter of quietly standing with him, supporting him. It is like the words from the Book of Proverbs:

A brother is a better defense than a strong city
and a friend is like the bars of a castle. (Pr. 18:19)

Sometimes, the only thing you can do in the presence of sorrow is mourn.

Tuesday, October 23rd

Kenny stopped at the door, and, before heading out into the October wind, called back to me.

"Father Gary, I have two words for you."

And I asked, "What would that be, Kenny?"

And he said, as he has so many times, "Love you."

What an unlikely place, in the gray of that day, in the bleakness of Commerce Street, to hear such words. But maybe the most appropriate place. His words are like arrows to the heart: straight and clean. This man touches me and teaches me about the heart and the power of the human spirit to communicate. Kenny sober, Kenny intoxicated, Kenny cracking jokes, Kenny weeping—in all cases his natural goodness sweeps me and my staff ahead of him. We are simply taken by his love; he crashes right through our walls and unleashes in us what is true and good. In just a few months, he is someone I have come to love.

Monday, November 19th

These past few days of getting away with the staff, a kind of retreat, have been healthy and productive. In the short time we have been together, Kevin and Beth (our two Jesuit Volunteer Corps members) and Joe and Terrie have taught me more deeply of the value of a team working together in the service of the homeless on the streets. I am learning from them the importance of believing in each other's talents and supporting one another's decisions.

We must learn the art of challenging each other in such a way which allows the recipient of our challenge (and our love) to grow and claim his or her life. We must be able to recognize the hurt in each other. There are times when we are disappointed or when we feel rejected or when we are having a rotten day. It is important to walk with each other in such moments. In a similar way, I hope we can learn to celebrate the successes of each other.

It seems to me that the notion of the Body of Christ will be better understood as I move and walk with my staff.

Saturday, December 15th

I received two memorable Christmas gifts today. Mary, a resident at a local supervised home for developmentally disabled, who comes in frequently, entered, cigarette dangling from her heavily-lipsticked mouth, gift in hand. Her face lit up like our Christmas tree lights as I opened the elaborate brown bag wrappings and found my gift of two—count them—two bars of Irish Spring soap. As if this weren't enough, she administered the coup de grace with a smacker on my cheek, marking me forever with an act of gift-giving.

The second gift came in two parts. First, with great fanfare by a straight-faced Bob, I was invited to come outside and receive my Christmas gift which "some of the guys" had put together. I should have suspected something. As I stepped outside, I received the second part: nailed with a flurry of snow-balls hurled by well-positioned snipers. It was the ol' "Let's-get-him-with-snowballs" setup. I tried to retaliate, but missed badly. I need lots of warm-up time before I can throw heat.

There is a simple joy to be found in the pain of the streets. It is as if the Spirit of God moves more freely at times, pouring out of individuals, trembling fresh. People who possess virtually nothing—no money, no power, no physical beauty—are often the authors of a kind of giving that makes me suck in my breath. There is something unmatchable—at a time when our culture swims in extravagance and conspicuous consumption—about the gift of bars of soap wrapped in a brown bag or the gift of unrestrained cackling over the launching of a successful snowball attack.

As I stood there, soap in one hand, brushing off the snow with the other, I looked up at some folks peering through the window from a nearby office building. They did not know whether I was crazy or whether I should be fearing for my life.

Wednesday, December 26th

We had a warm and wonderful Christmas Eve Mass, the little Nativity House full of our guests from the streets, many outside friends, and benefactors. I especially loved the time after we read the scripture when some people stood to give an expression of how they saw the birth of Christ. The devotion manifested cut across all the economic and social levels that were present. And, as is the tradition, we all shared in coffee and cookies after the service. It was a grand sight to see Little Joe, a rough-hewn, street-wise laborer of forty years holding court with three well-dressed folks from a local church.

One of the highlights of the evening was what I suppose I could call "The Kenny and Gordy Show." Around communion time, both men, a bit intoxicated, were arguing. It began as a low grumbling in the front row and evolved into a "candid" discussion of old friends. Kenny resented Gordy telling him to stop talking during this "most sacred" time of the Mass. At one point—the place in reverent silence except for these two characters—Kenny turned to Gordy and asked indignantly—for the whole place to hear—"What are you, some kind of a fucking captain?" I thought the little old ladies sitting behind them in the second row were going to faint, loose their teeth, or stomp out— or all of the above. Captain Gordy and his steamed Lieutenant Kenny calmed down when I gave them my mad-eyes. After Mass, they made profound apologies to me, to the staff and, of course, to the ladies, who neither fainted, lost their teeth, nor stormed out.

The poor, better than anyone else, understand the implications of being the child of homeless parents. In this case the parents are Mary and Joseph. And they understand that the decision for Jesus to be among the poor is a reflection of the heart and attitude of God. Jesus was born poor. He lived with the poor. He took his stand with the poor and sought to liberate them from the powers that oppressed them. Such acts the poor understand to be the acts of one who loves them.

Friday, December 28th

Sally was brought in today by some of our guests; she was shivering and hungry. She is mentally ill. Her brown eyes, probably in another time and place very beautiful, now expressed fear; it was the fear of someone who thought she was going to be abused once again. One comes to know that look down here, especially in the eyes of women.

How is it that there are so many physically and mentally ill people wandering the streets of America? How is it possible, in the times of billion dollar killer submarines and mega-buck professional entertainers? How is it that human beings can be forgotten, unprotected, unwanted, unrecognized? A child lost in suburbia is the object of a high-powered, to-hell-with-the-expense search. My God, a school of beached whales can mobilize entire federal and state agencies, not to mention thousands of whale-lovers. This country is full of Sallies, women beached on its sidewalks and gutters.

❖ *1985* ❖

Desperate Camaraderie

I am feeling wiped out tonight. I know that it is the fallout of the long and tortured discussion I had with Laura. She has that combination of qualities which the pimps of the world thrive on: drop-dead looks and low self-esteem. As we talked, she looked away with her uncommitted eyes, nervously pulling her hair, her lean, tall body now curling up on the chair, now uncurling. She cried a lot. She hates her job, hates herself, hates people.

Laura works as a dancer at one of the local strip tease joints. She makes extra money with "private showings" in a back room. Her life and her livelihood are bound to the presentation of her body. What is it like to be seen as a pair of breasts and a vagina? How can someone even approach the lowest rung of self-worth when the only compliment she receives is to be told that she is "a good piece of ass?" And what kinds of minds are we dealing with—what kind of sad, sick minds—that belong to the ogling males who fuel this whole travesty?

My stomach was churning during our conversation. I wanted to cross over into the land of her heart, but Laura has constructed a system of defenses that protect her heart from feeling anything. Her spirit hides because she is wounded. To be reduced to a commodity and the pleasure-object of leering strangers—who wouldn't be wounded?

I told Laura some hard truths: that her real beauty is inside, first and last; that she can only discover that beauty in the presence of men and women who care for her; that she is sacred because God created her this way; that her despair and anger were the flip sides of a person who longed to be tender and involved, who wanted to love and be loved. I also said that if she ever wanted to talk, I was around. There were moments when her eyes simultaneously teared and lit up, as if to say, "I want to believe this, but my life is so screwed up."

We talked for a couple of hours, oblivious to the noise of Nativity House. Trust me, Laura.

Sunday, January 13th

Just before we closed this evening, I received a phone call from Chico, a two-tour Nam Vet, frequently wired on heroin or booze, or both. He has a total disability as a result of the war, so he always has money to spend. He asked me to come and see him, so I wound up spending part of the evening in this seedy hotel room he had rented. He is always a bit paranoid, indeed, he never talks to me in Nativity House without his back to the wall. A little man, covered with morbid tatoos, he has a bandana around his head. Chico always anticipates trouble. Tonight, he was having some flashbacks, needed to talk, and he wanted to talk with me even though I am ignorant of the firsthand and grotesque specifics of that war.

Chico cares for me and for some of the staff and volunteers; there is a fierce loyalty to Nativity House manifested in warnings he gives to potential drug dealers who hang around or to anyone who might give us a bad time.

Tonight, there was a slow-building anger going on inside of him. He reminded me of a gigantic semi-truck moving inexorably through its many gears, heading toward that point of power and speed when the entire rig would be out of control, pulverizing anything that might obstruct it. In the middle of this build up, he became very embarrassed, excused himself, and went into the bathroom. There he fixed on some heroin. He came out, became very mellow, and eventually nodded off. After a couple of hours, assured that he was stable, I left, stepping out into a cold, foggy Tacoma night, praying for the peace and healing that Chico wanted. This is my role and my call too, connecting, in my prayer, the brokenness of a brother or sister human being with the power of a loving and gracious God. I make no claims as to how that works, but it is real and alive for me tonight.

Wednesday, January 16th

Even though we received some extra money for Christmas, my nature is to worry about finances in spite of my talk about trust in the providence of God. We have a modest budget, and I have a good Board of Directors out there hustling donations. So what's the big worry, Gary? Especially after today.

Beth came to me after the mail delivery, suggesting that I look at a particular piece of mail. It looked like another bill. In fact, it was a check for $10,000. A local business man, famous for his philanthropy, had slipped in Nativity House one morning, checked us out, drank some coffee. A few days later, he wrote out the big one for ten grand. It will give us a little breathing room until the spring and serve as a reminder of how easily I wimp out when it comes to this delicate business of trusting in God.

Thanks God. Love, the Wimp.

Saturday, January 9th

Two weeks ago Pete and I went out for coffee. He bought. Pete is a handsome, dark-haired man. This particular day he was treating me with some of the money earned working for a company that had hired him a month ago. His alcoholism had cost him dearly: family, friends, a profession on the East Coast. But he seemed to have turned it around. His intellectual gifts and his remarkable practical abilities promised a way to go foward in life. The guy was as comfortable talking about the psychology of interpersonal relationships as he was rebuilding a car engine.

It was a good talk, sprinkled with lots of the AA-type truisms like "God does not make junk," and other one-liners geared to reinforce a growing sense of booze-free dignity. We talked of my own family. Both of my parents were alcoholic. A lot of the gaps in my life and many of my personal struggles to grow and love myself can be attributed to living as a child of a mother and father who suffered from the disease. In his gentle and instructive way, Pete gave me a few tips on how to recognize and accept some of my pain and confusion and questions.

Today, his employer called me. My name had been used in the next of kin section in his application papers. Pete had left town, taking some company property and a bundle of company money. Later on, I found out through the usually reliable street grapevine that Pete had been drinking for the last few days and apparently had stepped off into the dark side once again.

I am sad and angry tonight. Sometimes, everything stinks.

Thursday, March 14th

A whirlwind day. Sometimes I had so many pans in the fire I would lose track of what tasks were to be done, and I had to work myself back through the list, so I could remember the first item. It was run and gun: I bandaged a bloody hand immediately after we opened; held a weeping Ace in my arms in the chapel, because he caught his girfriend in bed with his best friend; broke up a dispute between two people arguing over a guitar (should I be Solomon and cut it in half?); was asked by Candy if I could hold fifty bucks for her, and said, yes, I would, no interest charged; had a seventieth birthday for Ruth and sang her "Happy Birthday" over a cheapo cake taken from the freezer; took Ed, the Bus Buster, to the hospital after he slugged a bus that would not wait for him; asked Arnie to leave because he had lice, and told him where he could get a shower and proper medication; talked with Tony about his days as a prize fighter (he never fought a day in his life); spoke to Sherri who came in on a cane and had two black eyes, given to her by her boyfriend; helped Opal to the bathroom because she had wet her pants; talked to Francisco who called from jail and needed to see me right away, a matter of life or death; had one of our coffeee pots go out and found out that we were low on sugar; had J.W., all ninety-five pounds of him, threaten to "beat the living shit" out of a guy twice as tall and twice as heavy; carried the aspiring bantamweight, Giant J.W., outside and told him to take a walk for a few hours and cool down; had Jim ask me to help him with an employment application form; straightened out some guy who was constantly coming on to one of my female staff, and then he left very straight; met with the staff for a long and good review of the day after we closed. We were all pooped.

Friday, April 5th (Good Friday)

We had a simple religious service this afternoon with a small circle of staff and guests. There was Mark, a young alcoholic, three days into a tenuous sobriety, praying for his family in Oklahoma City; and Ric, the cool taxi driver with the dark glasses; Elizabeth, a local bag lady; two craggy old gentlemen who came in to "pay their respects"; a businessman dressed smartly in a three-piece suit.

Beyond these singled-out individuals there were many of the men and women guests whom we see frequently. Surrounding me, as I led the service, they brought their particular history of devotion to this day. The event and significance of Good Friday had been learned in their upbringing, in their travels, in their suffering, in their prayer.

What does it mean, this ancient commemoration of the Passion of Jesus, celebrated by this small band of believers? What strikes me is the importance of all of us being there, of creating the vehicle wherein our complex inner lives intersect with the story of the love of Christ. However dissimilar our lives may have been, we were bound together in those moments of faith. I was grateful to be part of this group today, there in this little storefront in downtown Tacoma. We were like the solitary flower on the mountain top; no matter how insignificant it is, surely it gives its own unique homage to God.

Kevin wrote this message in our spring newsletter anticipating the mystery of Holy Week:

So go our days, as the give and take of death and life flow out of and into each other. With only one window in our entrance not boarded up, we had a tomb-like quality. Contained within the tomb is the human cost of the slow death of alcoholism, prostitution, mental illness, the abandoned elderly, economic deprivation, loneliness. But, as in that long ago tomb in which Jesus rose through death to new life, there is, in our daily life here at Nativity House, the powerful truth that these deaths need not be the final word. We see the signs of life in the gifts of

spring flowers brought in by our guests, and by the care
that people share with one another.

Sunday, April 7th

Beth, Kevin, and I decided on an elaborate Easter Sunday
lunch of Campbell's Clam Chowder, augmented by a ton of
bread.

It was a disaster.

First of all, being the culinary experts that we were, we discovered that clam chowder required not water, but milk, and all
we had available was that killer USDA powdered stuff. So we
used it, thinking that we could make it real tasty. Then we burnt
the milk. Gallons and gallons of burnt milk. It looked like we
might have to go with Plan B: delicious cheese sandwiches.

We risked the shame and embarrassment of this so called
chowder. Wouldn't you know it, several of our guests, hands-
down experts on shabby meals, informed us that this soup was
arguably the best damn clam chowder that they had ever tasted.
I thought, "Very arguably, very arguably."

Maybe we could do a fundraiser, inviting the world to try
our "secret recipe."

In spite of the chowder crisis, it was a beautiful Easter Sunday with lots of sun and peace on the streets.

Thursday, May 2nd

Walking around the streets today, taking a break from the
noise and smoke, I came across Reggie sitting on a bus stop
bench. He was reading a book out loud because he was going to
a job interview, and he wanted to practice his diction. He was
an orphan. He was raised in a very tough area of New York City,
but came west to get away. He is fiesty, never one to back
down, reflecting a man who has had to make it on his own.

He invited me to critique his reading and pronunciation. So there we were, mentor and student, in our very unorthodox classroom on Pacific Avenue. Of course, I knew that the real teacher was Reggie, and I was the student. I was learning at the side of the headmaster, Reggie, learning of how life must be seized if we are going to make anything happen for the good. It was an impressive moment for me. I need to challenge myself when I back off or I am too lazy. Reggie taught me, too, to be bold in my confrontation with some of our guests who are ducking out on responsibilities to themselves and to others.

He returned later in the day just as we were closing. He got the job.

We loaned him bus fare for a week and promised a lunch to take with him.

This guy will make it.

Wednesday, May 15th

The ritual of fighting on the streets would be funny if it were not for the fact that people can be injured seriously, sometimes killed. Normally, if we are heads-up, we can prevent a fight before it reaches blows. I am learning that we must listen to hear the verbal preliminaries, be aggressive in separating the antagonists, and allow them to vent some angry words. It is important for people to save face on the streets. From our standpoint, too, as staff persons, it is important to bring along our sense of humor.

As Kyle was "stepping outside," to settle with someone who had said the wrong thing to him, I convoyed the two of them out the front door. Kyle's opponent took off his jacket very ostentatiously. Kyle, to my amazement, did not take off his coat, but took out his teeth and handed them to me. I felt like one of those characters called "seconds," who stands next to one of the principals in a duel. It was really quite funny, and everyone started laughing, including the jacketless opponent who was about to enter into mortal combat with Kyle. Standing there on Commerce Street, his teeth in my hand, I informed Kyle that I did not hold teeth—only guns, knives, brass knuckles, and, on occasion, a cold beer—and by the way, Kyle, how about not fighting at all. Both of the participants, out of "respect" for Nativity House, decided not to fight. So faces were saved and no damage done to bodies or to those yucky teeth.

Tuesday, June 4th

Tom, an unkempt, spaced-out mentally ill guest, became very agitated when I told him that he would have to go to the hospital to shower and be de-liced. He feinted as if to leave and then nailed me with a sucker punch. I went down, out cold. I awoke thirty seconds later, on the floor, surrounded by much noise and confusion. Kneeling in front of me, hands locked in supplication, was Doris, begging God "to please not let him die." From the back of the room ran Kevin, flying over me, intent on breaking up the gang of guests who had cornered Tom and were pummeling him for doing the unthinkable: taking a shot at Father Gary. Kevin and Beth were able to get Tom out of Nativity House more or less intact. As for me, I was groggy, but okay, surrounded by a host of Florence Nightingales there to insure my rapid recovery.

Violence is common on the streets, but the code around here is that one simply does not mess with the staff at Nativity House. In one sense, we are the most protected people in a world where people don't think twice about throwing a punch. Once there was a new kid on the block who was in my face over an issue of my preventing him from verbally abusing one of our guests. As we stood there, more or less nose to nose, we were surrounded by some of our biggest and meanest-looking guests. One of these self-appointed security guards said to the trouble maker, "His fight is our fight; you fuck with him, and it will be the last time you will fuck with anyone." I prefer to handle my own disputes, but it is good to know that there is backup. The message was clear to this fellow, and the code was observed.

There is a kind of justice that is enforced by street people when the innocent and weak and unprotected are being threatened or exploited. I am reminded of the prophet Amos who attacked those who oppressed the needy and crushed the poor. I have had local tough guys bring me wandering teenage girls, so that they will not be hustled by pimps. I have seen old and disabled men fly into the face of smart alecks who are picking on a mentally ill person. When I organized in Oakland, I remember how the most eloquent critics of injustice were those leaders whose roots were in the poor neighborhoods. The Spirit of God lives powerfully in the most obscure and with the most obscure.

Wednesday, June 26th

Gaunt, long-haired, attired in tattered dress clothes with a relic of a tie, sits Leo, our resident evangelical. A "former preacher," he comes in daily, his raggedy, heavily underlined Bible in one hand, his heavily made-up wife, Betty, held in the other hand. He is there at his table day after day like a kind, half-crazed John the Baptist, dispensing out religion to anyone who is interested. Most avoid him. Occasionally, like today, he becomes agitated because of someone's cogent argument against religion or by a nearby person's swearing. Once he is disturbed, he sort of snowballs into anger until, "overcome by the Holy Spirit," he becomes very loud and launches into what he calls "tongues." Unfortunately, his behavior never leads to any conversions, but, like ashes from a forest fire, he ignites all kinds of satellite yelling and screaming, most of which is some variation of "shut up."

We wound up this morning carrying him out to the street, one staff person under each one of his very thin arms. I told him outside that he would have to simmer down whereupon he responded, with all the pity and condescension of a believer talking to the uninitiated, how on earth could I expect him to control the Almighty Holy Spirit? Good question. Do you think then, Leo, that you could ask the Almighty Holy Spirit to calm down a bit? Well, yes, Brother Gary, he could do that. The Spirit eased up, and we returned Leo to his table, Betty in tow.

I love Leo. Those huge eyes that are always casting about are, in part, looking out for my staff, for me, and for all the little people that find their way into Nativity House. I have no doubt that the Holy Spirit dwells deeply and passionately within his great heart.

Sunday, July 14th

Mike, a long time ranch hand from Montana (his drinking finally led to a painful termination of the job), asked to talk with me this morning. His face was haggard, wasted, drawn. Last night, he had been raped at knife point. His attacker had pulled him into the recessed doorway of an abandoned building. How many times have I looked back into the face of someone crushed by the insane and indifferent violence that stalks the streets at nights? Here we are, human beings, capable of such goodness and tenderness, and yet something monstrous can exist in us. Mike and I talked, and eventually I convinced him to go to the hospital.

The slick thing about sin is that, even in its most ugly and dominating fullness, one can forget that it is around. On the surface, we protest that we have no problems, even though any honest fool has to admit that there is a screw loose in the human condition. And the screw can wobble and fall out. At that point, there are those unspeakable moments of terror which Mike experienced. What was done to him is a testimony to the interior chaos that sin produces.

As I ponder this horror story of flesh inflicted on flesh, I am aware of the real longing we all have for genuine human intimacy, for the desire to hold and be held, not in possessiveness, not in an act of destruction and self-indulgence, but in the fullness of care and respect and unconditional love. Does God weep over such a beautiful part of creation—the most beautiful part, a human being—which can so pathetically mutilate another and cast the victim aside like a chunk of rancid meat? Is not the mercy of God tested in the abuse that human beings pile on each other, whether it takes place in a recessed, skid row doorway or in the torture chambers of a totalitarian government or in cold acts of institutionalized racism or in the behavior of a greedy landlord? Your mercy, O God, has got to be your greatest attribute.

Honest love in confronting the complexity of this situation can appear to be simplistic and naive, but it must be the stand of Nativity House. I begin with Mike. Surely, whatever his grief and pain and anger, he must know that he can come here to weep and to be held in our arms.

Friday, August 23rd

One cannot be on the streets very long without meeting a Vietnam Vet. These men are a sad stream that continues to flow from that tragic part of American history.

Manuel, short, powerful, spent three years in Nam. He became a heroin addict there. Still is. He is a violent man and a gentle man, one of those weird paradoxes that is produced when a human being kills other human beings as a profession.

Jerry, thoughtful, sensitive, plays chess pensively in the corner of Nativity House. I always feel his rage under the serene exterior, although we have had no trouble with him. He told me that he lost the missing three fingers on his left hand to a sniper, and, looking me straight in the eye, he added, "My testicles were blown off by a grenade."

Tim has a body full of shrapnel and a head full of steel plates. He frequently helps out with the daily jobs like washing dishes and sweeping floors. He disappears periodically for several days at a stretch, not hiding the fact that this is when he drinks to oblivion in order to counter the reoccurring nightmares of the war, and the pain that pills do not alleviate.

Don matter-of-factly describes the killing and weapons of war. He told me of helicopter gunships that could turn a jungle floor full of Viet Cong into a green and red salad. Once he jokingly got into the brutality that was inflicted on the captured enemy, saying, "It was a matter of giving to them what they did to our guys." For Don, it was literally an eye for an eye, a limb for a limb, and a life for a life.

One could fill books with names and faces. And so here they are, these relatively young men, aged psychologically and spiritually in an instant on another planet. It is an instant that is forever played out in their minds. They wind up on the streets, victims of post traumatic stress disorder (PTSD), in all of its forms. At Nativity House, they can find a few of the brothers and sisters who are like themselves—people who know. Broken and handicapped and out of hinge with the society around them, they try to make it with each other. Like so much of the friendship on the streets, it is a desperate camaraderie.

We talk with them, we weep with them, we listen, reason, and pray with them. We hold them. We take them to detox centers and connect them with Nam rap groups and some of the emerging programs which the Veterans Administration (VA) is making available. We drive them to the hospital and to emergency rooms. We who are not Vietnam Vets are amazed at their drive to live (though suicide has claimed its grim toll), their capacity to endure suffering, their courage, and their dignity.

Whatever our ignorance of the war, Nativity House can offer the hope of human concern and no hassles, trying in our own way to meet the despair that is as real to them as the air. The raw truth of their experience brings out the best in our hearts. We know that even the best of love is tinged with self-seeking, but these vets purify our love.

There are many human beings that reveal Christ in his broken body. Surely, the Vietnam Veteran of the streets is one of them.

Thursday, September 19th

Urban development—so called—claimed the Colonial Hotel recently. It was a place of single resident occupancy (SRO), where some of the people that we see reside. Doug, a retired World War II veteran, who often helps us wash dishes, lived there. It was a cheap place to live; it was clean and decently administered; it was a hotel of single people, especially seniors who could not afford to live anywhere else. Its demise was rationalized by that two-edged sword called "progress," which slashes buildings and throats.

People outside of the street scene often ask me where the homeless are coming from. The destruction of the Colonial is a partial answer. When will urban policy makers and land use planners get their heads out of the sand and realize that the poor are being squeezed out of the housing market? Where on earth do they think SRO people can go, but to become part of the nameless army which trudges around from shelter to shelter, from substandard apartment to substandard apartment? Why should individuals have to suffer the indignities of inadequate housing in a country of such wealth?

The closing of the Colonial—and soon the Majestic—is an indicator that the street population will increase, and that affordable housing will decrease. It is a situation where buildings are being replaced, and human beings are being displaced. For a growing number of Americans, the dream is no longer to own a house; it is to find, for this very night, a place to sleep.

Saturday, September 28th

The new and old staff is now in operation. Kevin and Terri have returned and Marty and Marianne (members of the Jesuit Volunteer Corps—JVC) have joined us. Marianne had a run-in with one of the local drunks recently, a classic example of the gentle man who turns into a thug once he starts drinking. Today, he confronted her eye to eye and wound up blinking when she told him to leave. He said some rotten things to her, but to her credit, she told any would-be rescuers to back off, she would handle it.

Sometimes, in the confrontation with an obnoxious person who has been drinking, there is a temptation to be compassionate, especially if the person is sweet and kind when he or she is sober. It is an easy seduction for a novice on the streets who wants to help, and, for that matter, who wants to be liked by all.

But such compassion is misguided and naive. One simply has to be firm. I am learning that more and more. At the end of the day, after the staff review, we uttered a prayer for this man, praying for his healing, praying that our tough love will stay tough.

Tuesday, October 15th

A mentally handicapped woman, Gloria, walked into the office and said in her halting, stuttering voice, "I have bugs." Looking at her carefully, I could see the lice crawling out from underneath her cap. Later on, after the trip to the hospital, one of the nurses called me, her voice cracking over the phone. She said that this was the most raging case of lice that she had ever seen. It really breaks my heart. Gloria was like a sheep lost in the desert, so confused, dealing with something which she did not understand.

Disease on the streets is common and relentless. Each individual is faced with the problems of eradicating the disease. They lack finances, clean clothing, medication, rest, and food. They have a misplaced hope that the problem will go away. We have seen everything this year: venereal disease, tuberculosis, flu, pink eye, hepatitis, abcessed teeth, emphysema, boils, needle infections, scabies, heart disease, ear infections, blood-spitting stomach ulcers, chronic diarrhea, AIDS, severe athlete's foot—to name a few. This is to say nothing of the scraped, cut, banged, broken, ruptured, burned, bruised, sprained, kicked, slugged and otherwise untreated and injured arms and legs that people bring to us to us daily.

At the end of the day, I agonized over Gloria with my staff. We talked about it. Most people know that they have a physical problem. She does not. She is unable to protect herself. I felt helpless.

Monday, November 25th

We took Rose to the Greyhound Bus Station this morning. Destination: Montana and a better life. She pulled it out and pulled it off, working hard to get herself clean and free of drugs. The drug rehab program she completed has given her the space to claim her life. All the chaos of sexual abuse, of dope, of craziness and heartache—all of it is in her past.

It was a towering moment for all of us as we walked with her to the bus. She held each of us one more time in the twelve degrees of the still dark 7 AM. It was a simple act of gratitude, not uncommon with our guests; not a lot of words, just the non-verbal expressions of love and loyalty.

Monday, December 2nd

I spent part of the afternoon at the jail yesterday, talking with Major, a former Hell's Angel, who is now caught in the endless consequences of some bad and frantic choices. He seems to have a built-in button for self-destruction which he pushes periodically and winds up, yet again, in the slammer. He had a broken jaw, so our conversation was full of the hissing and slurring of squeezed words. I needed a translator with an expertise on words uttered through a smashed-up mouth. It was a couple of hours listening to a broken and confused heart.

Jail. What a scary place. I have been going to them for years, and they still get to me. Here, the poorest of the poor live. The jail is a big blob of concrete, bars, buzzers, glass, sterile halls, slamming doors, and cameras that endlessly watch you. From the moment I show my ID and begin the walk into the cell block, my stomach tightens up.

After my first visit in the Tacoma jail, I put the word out that anyone who wanted could call us—collect—at Nativity House. Sometimes, people need a favor; most of the time they just want to talk. The loneliness experienced in a jail is severe. It is with these brothers and sisters that Christ identified himself in the gospel of Matthew. I take some consolation in that gospel passage (Mt. 25) as I move through the halls and my fear.

Sunday, December 15th

A few days ago, Larry arrived. He is a super-character in a world of many characters. He has a marvelous and obnoxious laugh that pours out of his leathery, sun-soaked face, and he carries a ratty old guitar upon which he admittedly can play only one chord. He likes to call me "Dude," with a long *u* sound and sometimes extends that to "Dude-y, Dude, Dude." His one chord handicap is no obstacle to his bellowing out song after song—"all original," he tells me. The songs are so bad that I have to agree. He sang a song, especially dedicated and made up on the spot for me, assuring the surrounding audience that he never sings the same song twice. Larry is an audacious fellow.

There is a spontaneity about him which is irrepressible, a kind of charm that can win me no matter what he does. He is utterly himself, untouched by the rules of social conformity. Even the old vets around here, who have seen just about everything, smilingly shake their heads at this guy. He is some kind of Dude.

Wednesday, December 25th

We had a relatively quiet and prayerful Christmas Eve liturgy last night. Since lots of organizations and churches offer an all-the-trimmings-meal today at various locations in the city, we were not particularly swamped by people at our modest Christmas Day meal. People were quite excited by the gifts we were able to give to each. And a local candymaker gave us several cases of chocolate cream mints. Chocolate cream mints. On skid row. We pigged-out.

I looked around the room as the 100-plus guests were eating: old, young, male, female, all races. Many were jabbering away, others alone with their Christmas Day thoughts. I thought, as I pondered all my friends here, that all of us are in some way poor: economically, physically, emotionally, spiritually. Our poverty may not be obvious, but it is there; it is a condition of being a human being. Kevin once said that the greatest poverty is for a person to feel that they have nothing to offer, incapable of the gift of love. The consoling truth of the birth of Christ is that Jesus embraced us in our poverty by embracing our humanity; that God, made flesh, sanctified our life, each life, no matter how concealed or flawed, no matter how poor.

❖ *1986* ❖

Applying Hydrogen Peroxide

Wednesday, January 15th

I spoke to a local church organization two nights ago, to spread the word about Nativity House, and, hopefully, to raise a few bucks. I am still a little steamed by the lousy reception. From the look of the frowns when I came in and the subsequent hostile questions at the conclusion of my presentation, it was clear that they harbored very negative viewpoints about street people. If I could characterize their theology, it was from the school which holds that the Church should be about "spiritual" realities and should stay clear of "social issues."

It was a frustrating evening. I wonder how some Christians read the words of Jesus. It seem so obvious that Christ made the connection constantly between the love of God and the love of neighbor, and that his mission was especially directed toward the least, the abandoned, the outcast, the disenfranchised. Weren't the lepers and the prostitutes and religiously oppressed top priority for Christ?

The Church has to be in the market place. It must come out of the sanctuary. The poor that we see each day ask this question of the Church: Do you walk your talk? Do you preach from your pulpits about God's love for all people and then look the other way when there is a need to do something concrete for some of those people? Do you feed the hungry and clothe the naked and welcome the stranger (like some dirty street person) and visit the broken ones who are in jail?

As I was walking out of the church one of the members said to me, "Maybe some of those people get what they deserve." It was an arrogant remark to which I did not want to respond. I did think, though, of the line of Dorothy Day, the Catholic Worker founder, "God help us all if we got just what we deserved." I thought of how I would like to have kidnapped this Christian, who was so blithely writing off the homeless, and take him down to the steets, to the cheap hotels and the alleys and gutters and the shelters and to Nativity House. He needed to be around the cold and dirt and lice; he needed to see diseased body parts and smell bodily excretions and sewage. I wanted him to be around the noise of people who live crowded together,

33

never knowing the experience of privacy; I wanted him to meet people who eat their food prepared for hundreds or have grown up never having a sufficent food.

It was a sleepless night.

Sunday, February 9th

Angela and Dick had their baby last week. They are like so many young couples we see: struggling, poorly educated, surviving in the midst of poor-paying jobs, eviction notices, and tragic childhoods. They called me from the hospital happily informing me of the birth and telling me that they did not have enough money to take a cab home. Isn't that unbelievable? A new baby, a new mom and dad, and one of their first decisions, as new parents, was to figure out a way to get themselves and their child back to their crappy little apartment house.

I packed them into my car, trying to make as big a deal as I could over the babe and the proud parents. A few days later, they arrived at Nativity House to let many of their friends see, hold, and cluck over their son. Many, like the staff, had walked through the whole pregnancy with them. As I awkwardly held the naked Richard Jr.—his mother was fishing for a diaper—the little guy urinated all over me. It was, one might say, a good shot. There were lots of laughs as I nervously handed Dead Eye back to his momma and headed for the clothesroom in search of a clean shirt.

Monday, March 10th

Intimidation. Verbal intimidation. This guy, Kevin, is the Master. He has a Ph.D. in verbal games and verbal confrontations. As often as I tell my staff never to get into the angry word games of the streets (because they will be eaten alive), here I am again, today, taking on this man who can run circles around me. So much for the vaunted Jesuit education. At one point, he simply goes over the limit, calling me a fascist and a phony who is pimping the poor. I asked him to leave. As he went out, I was shaking inside, feeling totally out of my league. Hell, I was.

It gripes me that I allow myself to get trapped in arguments which I know will go nowhere. Why do I do this? And beyond that, how in the world do I love an adversary who shows me a face of implacable hatred and a fuck-you loathing? For all I have learned about the importance of staying with the issue in a discussion, it is so easy, in my fear and my desire to win, to become angry and get sucked into a verbal street fight in which I will never prevail.

Friday, March 21st

This long winter has left me tired. We have opened the windows a crack, and the open windows become a metaphor of the promise of new life on the streets. But right now, in all the sounds and smells, in all the sorting out and in all the high-octane stress of the streets this month, I cannot get into the promise of a new spring.

It is difficult to pray in the sometimes unsettling experiences of the day-to-day Nativity House. I am before you, O God, a little dumb and frightened. I am not frightened of you, but of myself. I feel inadequate in the face of so many problems I see each day, and in the knowledge of my limitations. I know, in faith, this does not matter to you. It never has. All you have wanted is a heart willing to reciprocate your love. I try to give that, but so often I love you and pray with one hand extended and the other one behind my back. I know that it is more than a life of periodically saying "yes" to you and doing things for you. It is a matter of a growing closeness, like any worthwhile and true love affair. I do not feel close right now. I am kind of just plodding. I suppose I feel sorry for myself. But we have talked these things over a jillion times before. Help me in what I do, to trust in your love through all the unresolved contradictions of my life. Help me through the winters. Open my windows. Again.

Thursday, April 24th

Leo died in his sleep. Kevin wrote these words a short time later:

We gathered at Mass and shared Leo stories in lieu of a homily. We laughed and cried as we remembered and gave thanks for this simple man of faith, who, in his own half-crazed way, had taught us much about God, love, and faithfulness. I have heard few people remembered better.

I thought of the words of an old folk song which celebrated the life of a tireless union organizer: "People like you help people like me go on."

Wednesday, April 30th

Three quick shots of love today.

Bobby, a chunky little old man between forty and eighty years, a little intoxicated, came in full of gloom because he had lost his wallet. Only fifteen minutes before, one of our guests had found the wallet on a couch and returned it to me. I gave it back to Bobby, and he proceeded to lay this big slobbery kiss on me, aiming for my face, but landing on my neck. He gave new meaning to the notion of an intimate kiss.

Next, I had asked someone to leave because of an attitude. He left, but not without punching the door jam right in front of me. For an instant, I thought he was going to hit me. In the tension that followed, as I was standing there, my heartbeat having quadrupled, Violet, a developmentally disabled woman who makes a daily appearance, came up to me. She always has an instinct for the staff and looks out for us in her simple way. She gazed at me with that unspeakable love which Violet has and offered me two chocolate chip cookies made recently by her boyfriend's mother. I accepted them gratefully and ate them in two nervous gulps as I took her into my arms.

Thirdly, Dolores, a traveling bag lady (she always shares with me a 1975 Portland newspaper article written about her), cornered me and insisted on singing to me her rendition of "Amazing Grace." No music critic in the world could have put her performance into words or described her purity of intention and depth of conviction. You are an amazing grace for me, Dolores.

Tuesday, May 25th

While I was talking with Vern and Cindy at breakfast, Vern suddenly stopped speaking. Then his eyes rolled back and his hands started quivering and, bam, he went crashing back on his chair—240 pounds and a table and Cindy all hitting the floor. It was a gran mal seizure. We quickly cleared the area around his violently contorting body and placed a pillow under his head. Every muscle in his body seemed to be thrashing; his whole system had gone into uncontrolled high speed. As we were trying to protect him and calm a hysterical Cindy, the paramedics were called. Slowly the seizure took its course, leaving the poor guy blitzed, dazed, and in need of rest.

Sometimes, there are people who fake their seizures for attention. We had two fakers last year who had some kind of strange rivalry going, so that when one was doing her best to crank up a petit mal, her competition was endeavoring to generate something on the other side of the room. They were famous with the paramedics. One of my staff tagged those occasions "The Days of the Dueling Seizures."

Seizures are so common down here, induced by alcohol, brain damage, or something inherited. Lots of folks forget or refuse to take the medication which normally can control the problem. It is very important for us to be present with the victims when they come out of the whole frightening experience. Besides being exhausted, there is always the embarrassment and that painful look on their face which says, "Did it happen again?" Life can be so fragile.

Friday, June 13th

It was a day of tension; maybe the unseasonal heat is getting to everyone. This morning, while waiting in the food line, Ernest, a pot-bellied, unemployed car mechanic, became angry with the guy in front of him, Barry, and hit the latter on the side of the head with an empty plate. Barry attacked. Even now, many hours later, I keep running it through my mind in slow motion.

Barry is a mentally disturbed man. He is an ex-convict, a former heavyweight boxer, who has this menacing-looking tatoo of a cross in the center of his forehead. He must have landed ten punches before the poor Ernest hit the floor, at which point Barry began to kick him in the head and body. First Kevin, my staff person, flew in to stop it; then I did, but we were thrown off like a couple of old rags. It did distract Barry, though, and at that point I was able to get his attention, move him back and try to convince him to leave. As he started to exit, he pushed me aside and started kicking Ernest again, then turned on Kevin and me. At that moment, out of the sky, a fellow by the name of Silver came to our rescue and threw a body block on the crazed Barry. Two or three others piled on, held Barry down, cooled him out, and then we were able to remove him from Nativity House. We immediately called the police and the paramedics.

The place was a disaster with blood and broken plates and overturned chairs everywhere. People stood around stunned, nervous. This man, Barry, had been like a locomotive out of control. Ernest was on the floor, moaning, and badly beaten up. I saw him at the hospital tonight. He has three broken ribs and the beginnings of two black eyes; they will be whoppers. He was in pain, but was, even at that point, able to reflect humorously, "I am usually more discriminating with whom I pick a fight."

Barry was subsequently arrested. In one of those strange twists of the Code, he called me (he was allowed one call) from jail and apologized, and, referring to Ernest, he added, "He shouldn't have hit me from behind, Father. People can get killed for that in prison."

My other thought on this is that Kevin and I owe a big act of gratitude to Silver, the long-haired and quiet man who intervened to protect us. He may have saved our lives.

Monday, July 21st

I received a phone call from Mark early this morning. He asked me if we could we get together and talk? I told him, of course. We met at a downtown coffee shop. He is a young man, twenty-five years old, extremely intelligent. For most of his life, he has battled alcoholism and today, gaunt from several sleepless nights, he needed to talk about his latest bender and what he wanted to do. Could I help him get into a detox/rehab center down in Olympia? This kind of question from the alcoholic inevitably places me in that world where I have to trust my instincts and play my hunches. Was he serious, or was this just a moment of decision that was fueled more by guilt and remorse than by the resolution that said, "This is it. I am turning it around"? My judgment was that he was ready. I was able to make some connections which enabled him to enter the rehab center in Olympia.

Coming back from Olympia, I reflected about how difficult it is to love ourselves, and yet how crucial this truth becomes when decisions are made to reach for health and sanity. Mark has to bite the bullet and reach for whatever it is deep inside. Arthur Miller's line, in his play, *After the Fall*, comes to mind: "There comes a time when one must take oneself into one's arms." It is true. I can love Mark, his family can love him, the best alcohol counselors in the business can offer their help and care, but in the end he must make the choice for himself. Yet even that is tough. Alcoholism is a monster whose most insidious weapon is the power to erode even our judgment. In these moments I hope in the mercy of God and the power of grace to overcome the most entrenched course of self-destruction.

It is painful witnessing this kind of honest struggle. I am aware once again of my parents and their battles with alcoholism. In the same breath, however, no matter what the debilita-

tions of the disease, they gave me life and a fundamental sense of
what is valuable and good. A lot of hope is found in that observation about myself, and I carry it instinctively into my relationships with the alcoholics of the streets. It is like Paul says in
Second Corinthians, there is strength in my weakness.

Monday, August 11th

Uncle Albert, the undisputable king of the panhandlers, is
moving more slowly these days and talking of death. I wonder
if he is finally turning the corner and heading for the end. He
told me once that he drank two bottles of Thunderbird before
nine in the morning just to get going for the day. How can anyone beat up their liver like that and survive?

He is a former businessman from California's San Joaquin
Valley, a self-proclaimed "gray-haired old fart," who seems to
have resigned himself to a no-turning-back, drink-till-I'm-dead
philosophy.

He is also very intelligent and clever. Once I kicked him
out for a week, and for the entire time—in the cold February
wind—he proceeded to sit cross-legged in front of Nativity
House. It was a public retribution for my unjust decision. Another time, when I simply had had it with some obnoxious behavior and threatened to call the police if he did not leave, he
proceeded to the phone and made a 911 call, reporting, "I would
like to inform you of a so-called priest who is, at this very moment, harrassing me."

Yet in all of our showdowns, there exists a tenderness between the two of us. He wept one day in the office when word
reached him that his 83-year-old mother had died in Fresno. His
tears were a sign, of course, of the love a son has for his mother,
but, given the fact that he was crying in my presence, they were
also a kind of self-revelation which very few of his acquaintances
had ever witnessed. The honesty of his tears were a gift to me.

Saturday, September 13th

"How long does it take to become a human being?" asked Joan despairingly as she told me the story of her three sons who will not have anything to do with her. One had apparently told her over the phone last night that she was not even a human being as far as he was concerned. Sometimes, it is a terrible burden which the people of broken relationships must carry.

Stacy, one of the new staff persons this fall, said it well as she was reflecting on how difficult it can be to walk with someone who is suffering: "At some point, all I wanted to do was hold this guy in my arms."

We talked about it in our daily staff review today after we closed up.

Of course this cuts to the heart of the problem: what path do you take when you are in a position of helping someone on the streets? People are so vulnerable, and the love that is offered can be misinterpreted. Beyond that, there are many individuals who see the willingness to listen as the prelude to yet another rejection.

How can we stand in the breach of the broken lives which we touch? How can we take risks for the sake of our hurting brothers and sisters? I pray that we will be given the skills of a discerning heart.

Wednesday, September 24th

It rained all day today and was a bit brisk for September. A bearded, rain-soaked fellow walked in, carrying over his shoulder an unconscious man whom he had found lying in a gutter two blocks down the street. Calmly he said, "No cars were stopping, so I brought him here. Can you give him some soup or something?" He laid the sick man gently on the floor and waited with us until the paramedics arrived. The initial diagnosis was malnutrition and what was probably pneumonia.

The bearded one sipped some coffee, then bade us farewell, saying he had to catch a ride down at the trainyards. Destination:

Idaho. He gave us no name, only his exquisite act of human care.

And Jesus asked, "Which of these three, do you think, proved himself a neighbor to the man who fell into the brigands' hands?"

"The one who took pity on him," he replied to Jesus.

Saturday, September 27th

Skinny Lynn has been in town for the past several days. He wanders between Portland and Seattle, lives off Social Security Disability checks, and uses heroin when he has any money. He has a very sad early history of abusive foster parents and looks older than his thirty years. In spite of all the hardships that have been inflicted upon him, or that he has inflicted upon himself, he has a winsome way and a loyalty to the staff and Nativity House. It is a joy to see him come through the doors and greet each one of the staff persons. He never forgets their names. He is a gabber, loves to talk about sports and who is playing whom, and what the betting line is on the games of the day.

He has a ridiculous kind of fearlessness at times, but one born of a lifetime of being on the defense. From his perspective, life is a matter of attacking or being attacked. Today, three drifters were in for lunch and began giving him a bad time, directly in front of the kitchen where I was helping to prepare the meal. One of them, a big-boned guy, started garbage-mouthing Lynn, calling him a faggot, and made a move to grasp him by the throat. The guy was eight inches taller and probably outweighed Lynn by a hundred pounds. Before I could break it up, Lynn, like an angry cobra, had pushed Mr. Big Mouth away and nailed him with a punch flush on the jaw. The big drifter went reeling into a nearby wall and had that blank look of someone who never knew what hit him. It surprised me to see Lynn capable of such strength. I got to Lynn quickly as the other two drifters began to make their move, and I literally picked him up and carried him to the chapel. The staff moved all three of the trouble makers outside, one of them moving very slowly. Together, they would have destroyed Lynn, but even then, as they were leaving, he was shouting over my shoulder, jabbing the air with his finger, daring them to come and fight him, almost as if his life depended on making a point. In a sense, it did.

Inside the chapel, Lynn went from white-hot rage to a fearful, small boy, weeping in my arms. It was a dramatic change. It is hard to imagine a life of constantly looking over your shoulder, going from moments of survival to moments of lonely fear. As we talked he said to me: "Sometimes I feel like all of us on the streets have been kidnapped from somewhere—some other world—and dropped here by a helicopter. And we are all trying to get out."

Friday, October 10th

Yesterday, Vicki, a hooker who occasionally works the downtown streets, came in, asking if she could get some clothes. It was clear that she was hurting. In the clothesroom, I asked her to remove her sunglasses which she did reluctantly. Her face was hamburger. Some trick had beaten her up, raped her, and kicked her out of his car. She can't "work" for awhile she said anxiously which of course implied that there would be no drugs from her slime-bag pimp.

It was important at that moment of clothesroom companionship to be present to her. No summit conference had more at stake in terms of establishing trust between participants. At 25, Vicki was caught in the madness of prostitution and drugs, and right now, she was grasping for some meaning in the chaos of the madness. She was not in Nativity House to obtain clothes. Rather she needed to talk, to stand quietly someplace where she could be free of judgment, to know that, maybe, there was someone who cared.

For Vicki, there was a mountain of personal problems. We talked about them as I was gently applying hydrogen peroxide to some facial cuts.

She left with a request to talk again and a comment that I should have been a doctor.

Thursday, November 11

I am taking a few days break here at Nestucca, a re-
treat/sanctuary in Northern Oregon, leaving Stacy, Neil, and
Marianne to hold down the fort. I woke after a night of fierce
dreaming, including one sequence involving Tiny, a midget
whom we see occasionally at Nativity House. He slides around
the edges of small-time street vice. Tiny and I talked in the
dream although I do not recall the exact nature of the conversation. I feel like Tiny sometimes, very small, finding it difficult to
reach the heart of many of our Nativity House guests. On the
other hand, I am consoled to know that many see the love on
my face and the faces of my staff. What is it that the Psalmist
says in Psalm 43? "Deep is calling to deep." We are all the same
height when it comes to one human being talking to another
human being, all the same height from the viewpoint of God
who created us.

I have been reading once again some of the writings of Dorothy Day, always inspired by her lived-out conviction of the connection between the love of God and the love of the poor. She
never stopped with pious remarks about our need to love the
poor, but related the reality of poverty to its causes: a world ob-
sessed with armaments, a government with priorities that often
gave second and third-rate attention to unemployment, lack of
educational opportunities, poor housing, and the scandal of in-
sufficient health care for those who cannot afford it. And as
much as she loved the Church, she never stopped reminding it to
march into the marketplace and fight for the right of the economically oppressed.

Saturday, November 29th

We have had a phantom bathroom guerilla of late, a person
who specializes in toilet plug-ups, using all kinds of things: ap-
ples, styrofoam cups, cigarette packages, old shorts, great gobs of
toilet paper. To have a jammed toilet here, one of the few bathrooms that is available to street folks, is big trouble. This indi-

vidual also dabbles in grafitti, likes to pour water over the dry toilet paper rolls and—being an accomplished plumber—will frequently unscrew the pipes under the sink.

Among the other talents that the staff has had to develop is how to plunge or repair a toilet and, more importantly, a nose (so to speak) for the perpetrators of Nativity House bathroom capers. In the latter case, what do you look for? Someone who talks obsessively about bathrooms? A person who hates toilet paper? Or maybe someone who hangs around bathrooms and just likes to tinker around with all of its parts? We once had a guy who could not stay away from electrical outlets and fixtures, who was forever plugging and unplugging the coffee pot, not to mention turning lights off and on. Or is this guerilla just creating a diversion, poised to trash the chapel when our attention is elsewhere?

I know we'll get this individual; all of our guests have an investment in solving the mystery. We will—aaaa—flush the culprit out.

Tuesday, December 2nd

I have just returned from a few days of retreat and reflection with the staff. This is a good staff, honest, open, alive, and loving. Whatever the difference in our ages, they bring a lot of wisdom to me and keep me reaching. They are a prayerful and playful bunch, even as they are consummate activists, activists who love the people they serve, and in whose presence they grow. It is a fine thing that Nativity House can say of itself that Neil, Stacy, and Marianne are here.

As Director, I try to wear many hats with my staff. I am a mother, father, brother, friend. I have to know when to listen carefully and when to talk; when to be a teacher who can speak to the issues of the human heart and the sociology of the streets. I want to strive to be a student who can learn from my staff's observations and experiences—of their own personal lives and their professional lives at a street drop-in center. I need to know when to challenge and when to back off, when to be a psychologist who can move with some of the debilitating moods of a staff person (moods that we all have), and gently call them to the higher ground of their willing hearts that are only momentarily jammed. I want, in faith, to see our mission here as an enterprise that is, ultimately, inspired and sustained—materially and spiritually—by God. In God's Providence, these people—these staff people—are here to assist in the grand enterprise of bringing God's love to the poor and to the marginalized

Above all, it is incumbent upon me to believe in the uniqueness of each one of my staff, that each brings something special to our guests, and that he or she must be given the space to claim their talents and their own kind of human love. And therefore, I want always to be on guard not to rob them—by some premature intervention—of the chance to use their gifts, whether such use may lead to failure or success.

Saturday, December 20th

Marianne wrote the following in our Christmas newsletter to the Friends of Nativity House.

Christmas often brings a lot of warm images to our mind, but the reality of the Nativity scene was probably quite different from the one we hold on to. It may have been cold, the stench of animals unpleasant, with Mary's pain and Joseph's fatigue compounding the fear and insecurity as they faced their awesome responsibility. What remains true, no matter which sense we look at, is that our God chose to come to earth, not as a powerful, heroic figure, but as a poor, humble, homeless child.

Today, there are still lonely, damp, uncomfortable places filled with people mystified as to what has brought them together. At Nativity House, we hope to take some of the chill out of the air and soften the harsh reality which pervades life on the streets. As in the story of the manger, Nativity House is often portrayed as a place flowing with goodness, wholesomeness and charm. What is forgotten is the daily struggle for food, clothing, sanity, and friendship which our guests endure.

Set apart from the whirlwind of activity which consumes society, the simplicty here allows the focus to be on one another. This enables us to see beyond our own circumstances into each other's hearts, and respond from our own. As we discover the gift of the individual, the loving, mysterious atmosphere of Nativity House appears. It is a living spirit, but it only comes with personal contact.

❖ *1987* ❖

Angel and Wingnut

Tuesday, January 20th

Neil spends long hours with Ladonna, a wispy, silent bag lady with sad eyes. She lives down the street in a cheap hotel room and comes in, usually on weekends, for meals and long hours of sitting. She has this little push cart that is always filled with a weird variety of items; I always remember the roller skates. On occasion, she will pull out a couple packages of Camels and sit there, distributing them to the many takers. Free cigarettes down here go like popcorn at the movie—fast.

I asked Neil what was happening in the periodic conversations he has with Ladonna where it appears that he is talking and she is not acknowledging his presence; rather she is looking off in space or at another one of our guests. As many times as they have talked, I am sure she doesn't know his name, although she once called him Clark Kent in a brief burst of words. And yet she never leaves, never gets up and walks away as she has done countless times with me. Neil explained to me saying, "It is important to be present. Maybe someday she will turn to me and say, 'So, Neil, how the hell are you?'" Someday. Maybe she already has in that mysterious inner world. Deep calling to deep.

I know, even as I ask such a question of Neil, there is a deeper part of him that is responding to Ladonna. He believes in her, believes that she is worth his best gift giving. It is important to be faithful to her. He knows we all long to have someone believe in us even when we are tied up in ourselves. Ladonna, sitting in her silence, is always teaching.

Thursday, February 17th

At 2 AM I was called to the local shelter, a place where the folks of the street can stay overnight. Someone had overdosed on something. Coming into the shelter, it was a pathetic and eery scene: sights of simple bunk beds and agitated people, the smells of unwashed bodies and death. At that hour, certain realities were intensified: I could feel the aloneness, the despair, the failure. The police and paramedics were finished because the man was dead. People were milling around, and there was the unreal scene of two men playing cards off in one corner. Moving around in the 100 or so people was Randy, a potentially explosive young man. He paced back and forth, mumbling to himself. As much as he had seen death in his life, there is a point of too much, even for the hardened. Apparently, the dead man had died in the bunk below him. I spent some time with Randy and a few others, trying to calm things down.

No one knew the dead man.

To die alone. To die alone and homeless. To die alone, homeless, and totally unknown. It wrings me out every time I witness something like this. And it is a drop in the bucket when one looks at the national figures of homelessness and talks to people who work with the homeless population. Part of me switches off, a defensive reaction to the loss of yet another human being by drugs, violence, old age, suicide, alcoholism, needless accidents, a broken heart. Part of me switches on, as it did when I moved among my friends at the shelter, being some kind of weak lightning rod of life and hope in the bleak world of those early hours. It was a moment of raw and stark faith, all the trappings of religion stripped away. I was Peter walking across the waters.

The dead man was taken away. This morning at Mass someone whispered his name in our prayer, a name since discovered. We give you, Holy God, our brother, Ray. Now, at last, let there be peace.

Wednesday, March 4th

Little Big Man is just that: little, about five foot, three inches, and big, which is to say that he is seemingly indestructible in a life of fighting that goes all the way back to the Korean War. I am sure that something went haywire inside of him in that war. He possesses a quick, jump-start willingness to fight, especially when he has been drinking. His short fuse gets lit when someone has offended his sense of fair play. He was apparently a boxer at one time, so not somebody to be taken lightly. In spite of this pugnacious quality, he has a disarming personal candor and loyalty, manifested in these great flourishing embraces where he buries his head into my chest or when he leaps to the protection of a staff person.

Today, in a snit over an alleged insult, he took a swing at someone whereupon we kicked him out for the day. Two minutes later, Little Big Man returned, an empty bottle in hand ready for action. We kicked him out and called the police. He returned with a two-by-four. We kicked him out again (he will not take on the Nativity House Staff—the Code is always operative). He returned swinging a large plastic bag full of someone else's clothes. He was kicked out once more as the police arrived.

As they were driving away, Little Big Man, sitting handcuffed in the back seat of the squad car, yelled out the window to me, "I wouldn't hurt that guy in Nativity House out of respect for the place and God, but when I get the mother-fucker outside, I'll kill him."

Sometimes, the little-son-of-gun is a pain in the fanny, but in spite of it, I like him.

Friday, April 17th

Good Friday. Every year we have a special service on this day, cleaning up a bit early and and putting the word out that all are welcome to come and pray with us. I looked around for someone to read a passage from Isaiah, and Marlon volunteered. He is Canadian, comes through periodically, a very artistic man, a quick sense of humor that reflects his great intelligence. His life has been a series of disastrous episodes with alcohol, yet ironically there have been long stretches as an alcohol counselor. He has been in and out of some hard drinking since he hit town, but today is sober, pensive, quiet.

There came that point in our Good Friday Liturgy where he began to read; his face was dirty, a bit bloated. The clothes he wore indicated that he had more than likely slept out last night in a doorway or in an empty field. Appearance-wise, he was a

mess. As Marlon read, slowly—so slowly that it was spellbind-
ing—but with a clear strong voice, the gathered group of wor-
shippers became more hushed with each line. He was reading
Isaiah's prophecy of the Suffering Messiah, and I think everbody
knew that he was reading a description of himself:

> As the crowds were appalled on seeing him—so disfig-
> ured did he look that he seemed no longer human—so
> will the crowds be astonished at him, and kings stand
> speechless before him; for they shall see something never
> told and witness something never heard before.
>
> Without beauty, without majesty (we saw him), no looks
> to attract our eyes; a thing despised and rejected by all
> people, a man of sorrows and familiar with suffering, A
> man to make people screen their faces; He was despised
> and we took no account of him. (Is. 52:14-53:3)

It was as if Marlon were the incarnation of the very words
that he was reading.

At the end of the service, we sang an old spiritual, "Were
You There When They Crucified The Lord." From off to the
side, this magnificent baritone voice made itself known,
forcefully, beautifully and, for sure, passionately. It was Monroe;
Monroe, who the police had brought in earlier in the day. They
had found him wandering in some downtown alley, a little tipsy,
but harmless. He is a kind man, a veteran of World War II,
where he lost his leg. Frequently, he carried his artificial leg
around, stuck through his crutches. So there he was singing his
heart out, very sober after an afternoon of drinking coffee. I
thanked him after we finished, grateful for his contribution to
our so-so singing. He responded with words that I shall never
forget, because they had so many levels of meaning in life, in
friendship, on the streets: "Just tryin to back ya, Father, just tryin
to back ya."

Sunday, April 19th (2 AM)

At the Easter Vigil tonight, Kevin was baptized. He is a long-time friend of Nativity House, a fellow who just wandered in a few years back and comes in to help us all the time. He is a Nam vet, and the injuries he suffered have left him with a big disability, but they have not diminished his good heart. Just before I baptized him in a ceremony in which he would be totally emersed in the baptismal fount, he looked at me and said, "Slam dunk me three times, Chief." I did.

There is a great affection between Kevin and me. He calls me "Chief" because he is forever giving nicknames to people and figured this is the most appropriate for the boss of Nativity House. It has a deeper meaning. It is the title he gives me because I am one of the most important people in his life. He knows he can count on me and knows that I will always be truthful with him, even when he does not want to hear the truth.

Saturday, April 25th

I had one of those exhausting philosophical discussions that occurs periodically. It was a three-way conversation involving Robert, Bill, and me. Robert is a young Nam vet, very burned out on substance abuse, and Bill is mentally ill, but functional, living in a group residence. Bill loves to talk about the elaborate schemes which the federal government has devised to get into his brain. Both men are very smart.

Today, Robert was trying to establish a metaphysical point that all which exists was intrinsically evil. His position was fueled, I'm sure, by his experiences in Vietnam. Bill was racing back and forth into his epistemological theories which proved that our brains were so messed up that there was no way we could even make judgments about the goodness or evil of reality. I was the existentialist in the discussion, appealing to reason, and to our ability to take our stand in life, to differentiate between good and evil, and to face the hostile world around us with the exercise of our free will.

There we were, the three of us at the Philosopher's Corner, sipping our coffee and smoking cigarettes. In one sense, it was hilarious; these two guys were like loose cannons on the philosophical deck, not really concerned about making a point, but rather more interested in firing and getting my reaction. On the other hand, there was a deeper agenda—for both of them—something, I believe, that existed below their separate illnesses: a desire to talk about their search for meaning with someone they could trust.

Wednesday, April 29th

As I was standing on the street this evening out in front of Nativity House, Dennis and Tio came to me, one on either side, and gave me a grand hug. Both had been drinking, so their affective inhibitions were gone. Normally, at the end of the day, given my fatigue and the tasks that need to be sorted out before leaving, I would have ignored them, gently fending them off. But it struck me that there was a great love here, and this was their moment to express it; a moment of boldness, guards down. I dislike their alcoholism, and I know that it will kill them at a young age, unless they change their behavior. Still, I never want to be indifferent to the overtures of any human being on the streets, including, and maybe, most especially, those of the alcoholic and drug addict. It is so easy to be blind to the various forms of expressed love because we are busy casting judgments on the givers of that love.

I took the two small men into my arms. I wanted them to know that I loved them too.

Friday, May 1st

There is a Native American woman, worn down by physical abuse, alcoholism, and malnutrition who has been coming in of late, usually making a beeline for Stacy whom she embraces and takes to some corner for a prolonged visit. I think of this scene as I read some of the words that Stacy wrote in our spring newsletter:

> The women we come to know at Nativity House are often involved in a struggle to maintain dignity and a sense of self-worth amid a cycle of poverty and abuse. These women of broken down bodies enfleshing hearts have touched us with their nurturing spirit and strong gentleness.
>
> Their weakness is their strength. It seems the broken ones reach out to touch others with great gentleness because of their own pain. We learn from them that those who society defines as powerful can deny that which means life, but they cannot give life. It is the weak, the broken, the victimized who reveal, in the vulnerability of their lives, what it is that gives life.
>
> In the Book of Wisdom there is a description of the women I have come to know and love: "She is the reflection of the eternal light. . . . She renews the world." (Wisdom 7:26-27) They live out this irony: in lives that are seen as dark, some light shines through to those they come among. They renew us in our longing to be held in the warmth of authentic love.
>
> Christ, like a mother, longed to gather the broken ones to himself—to soothe the pain, to heal. At Nativity House we are given the opportunity to share with Christ this strong element of the feminine spirit. It is by the grace of the Spirit and those around us, like the homeless women, that we learn to hold each other's words and persons gently.

Sunday, May 3rd

A Jesuit friend of mine came by briefly today. John was on his way back to California after attending a meeting in Seattle.

We go back almost thirty years in the Society of Jesus, and, although we are involved in different kinds of work in different parts of the country, we have kept in touch over the years. It was good to visit over coffee in spite of the usual noise of Nativity House. Of course, many of our guests were curious who John was. Several of them asked me later, after John had left, if he was my brother. I said no, not a blood brother. Our relationship was much deeper than blood brothers.

As I reflect tonight over the visit with John, my thoughts turn to the Jesuits as a group and my life within that group. I remember my mother, not a Catholic, periodically asking me how the Jesuits were different from the Catholic Church. I explained to her that the members of the Jesuits were Catholics, although there had always been critics of the Society of Jesus, and that could confuse the issue. I told her that there have been attacks made on the Jesuits over the years both from within and without the Church, all in the name of some abuse that the Jesuits had allegedly inflicted on orthodoxy. Mom always resolved these weighty matters in the pure light of her affection for me and the few Jesuits she had met. She knew we were good people; ultimately, for her, this knowledge rendered all controversies meaningless.

I have a great affection and care for the Society of Jesus. On the personal level, the Order has been the vehicle which has brought some wonderful people into my life. It has given me an education which most would envy. The Jesuits challenge me to listen to Christ, to follow him and to work to bring Christ's longing for peace and justice into the world.

But the Jesuits are not this big loveable machine. It is the individuals who make the difference. We are certainly a mixed bag of individuals. Some of us are Olympic-level jerks, and some of us are class acts. There are those whose brilliance is stunning, and there are others of average ability. I know some Jesuits, scattered thoughout the world, whom I count as my dearest and best friends.

From my brothers in the Society of Jesus I have learned much. Some great principles and values stand out: the importance and joy of enduring friendships; the value of prayer and to act out of that prayer; the ideal and importance of Christ as the center of my life; the search for a deeper commitment to the poor; the need to have a world-wide perspective; the goal of bringing a Christian perspective to social structures; the principle of adaptability to changing times and cultures and subcultures; the daring to risk, to take a chance, to experiment, to make things happen; the importance and exhilaration of building community.

It is true. We are more than just blood brothers.

Sunday, May 17th

Harold, tall, gentle, sensitive, and college-trained book-keeper, has been here for several months. He told me today, tearfully, that he has tested positive for AIDS. Harold is gay. It was all so sad, so full of anguish. He is a good man and has an unaffected holiness about him. The staff appreciates him for his loving presence and willingness to help us out in some of the behind-the-scenes jobs of Nativity House, like washing dishes when we are pushed for time. He has decided to return to Seattle where he can join an AIDS support group, as well as continue the progress he has made in Alcoholics Anonymous. We will miss him. I wonder if we shall ever see him again?

Some, like Harold, who have this terrible disease, seem to be willing to face their affliction straight on and make the changes in their life which will ensure a prolongation of life as well as the protection of others. I have met some individuals, though, who are bitter and vindictive. Not too long ago, I talked at length with a young prostitute who had been infected by one of her customers. She continued to work the streets, having sex without protection, taking a cynical and angry stance, saying, "They will get what they deserve." AIDS had become not only that which would kill her, but an instrument of revenge. I cannot reach her. I feel helpless.

Friday, May 22nd

June simply lost it today. She is a big woman whose mental illness is more or less held in check if she stays on her medication, but if she goes off it, which she apparently has, there occurs an outbreak of uncontrolled fury. She has a crush on me, but her anger is generally directed toward women, especially women who are perceived to be close to me. Sure enough, when Stacy was moving among our guests today, serving lunch, June hauled her down from behind. Fortunately, some of our folks were there right on the spot. They extracted Stacy's hair from the crazed grasp and removed her, very shaken up, from underneath a ranting and raving June. And it was not over because when the police and the people from the Tacoma Mental Health Department arrived, she proceeded to attack them. They finally took her out, strapped face down in a stretcher. As she was leaving, I had this feeling that she was glad she was being taken to the hospital—again.

It is scary to experience the rage that exists on the streets, especially as it lives in the mentally ill. If I am killed at Nativity House, or one of my staff, it will probably be at the hands of a disturbed person who has put on us the face of some tormenting demon. It is my most lingering fear for my staff.

Saturday, June 6th

A friendly, frail Englishman introduced himself to me recently. His name is Arlon. He's probably in his mid-fifties. He is a talkative person, usually on the manic side, and my hunch, from the first moment of our meeting, was that he had some mental problems. He tends to be a bit self-righteous, in a cheerful sort of way. When I disagreed with his line of thinking on some theological issue, he accused me of having a prejudice toward those who do not think like I do. He may have had a point. I subsequently have learned that he worked for Boeing at one time, an engineer, and, in the midst of some domestic problems and professional pressure, proceeded to snap. His arrival on the streets of Tacoma came shortly after his release from Western State Hospital. He has all those gentlemanly qualities that one associates with British royalty.

The other day I saw him standing on a bus bench on Pacific Avenue, singing his heart out and waving at the passing cars. The wags of the street refer to him as a "wingnut," a term that is jokingly applied to the mentally ill. But he is a happy wingnut and one who can touch my heart. Mae, one of our long-term and dedicated volunteers, who has come in for years and knows plenty of the people on the streets, refers to Arlon as an "angel." In the sense that an angel is defined as a messenger of God who brings the unexpected, I am beginning to think that the two titles of angel and wingnut are synonymous.

Friday, June 19th

Uncle Albert died today. Cirrhosis of the liver.

I was able to see him at the hospital last night, just around midnight. He was all tubed up, but semi-conscious. Albert was always pretty cynical about religious things, but I asked him if he would like me to say the Lord's Prayer. He did not respond. Then I rambled on about the time he had called the police on me and—to my surprise—he gurgled a laughing response. Thinking that this was about the only way he could communicate, I asked if he would like me to pray with him and, if so, please laugh again. He did, his eyes saying "yes." That was the scene: Gary, the professional religious, and Albert, the professional cynic, hunkering down for some old-fashioned death bed prayer. He may have acted like a cynic, but he knew that I knew that underneath all that tough street exterior was a big fat marshmellow. He dozed off in another fifteen minutes, and I left, asking that I be notified if there was any change. He died four hours later. I love you, Albert, my cantankerous old friend.

Friday, July 10th

Cops. To this point of my three years here at Nativity House, I think my relationship with the police has been a matter of disdainful toleration. It is an attitude, for my part, born of a number of things. I resent their ho-hum demeanor when they are checking out some violence in or near Nativity House as if to say, "Well, really, what the hell can you expect of a bunch of bums and a renegade priest." I resent the swaggering way they often make an entry, never bothering to acknowledge me or my staff, even though our friendship would help their job, not to mention put them at ease. I resent an apparent condescension to many of the brothers and sisters of the streets whose appearance is taken to mean a second class kind of citizen.

Today, one of the local beat cops, who has a big chip on his shoulder, unleashed his anger, accusing me of making his job extremely difficult. He was griped because I would not give him some information dealing with a particular individual on the streets. I countered, of course, that there is information given to me in confidence, and maintaining that confidence took priority over his need to have the information. What a scene, there on the sidewalk in front of Nativity House, the policeman and his rookie partner scolding me. I responded that I did not need to take their language and asked them for their badge numbers. I told them that I would take the matter up with their superior officer.

The gathered street people, of course, loved the whole showdown: it was Luke Skywalker against Darth Vader; the Good Guy against the Meanies.

In the end, as the steamed cops were walking away, one of them made the mistake of telling me that he had been on the streets for quite a long time, as if to say he knew more than I did. "How long," I said to myself, "Eight months?" I then told him, "Officer, I was on the streets when you were still a little kid."

It was probably a stupid, clever, and snot-nosed remark on my part, but, God, it felt good.

Monday, July 20th

There is new drug on the streets, a derivative of cocaine, called crack, a small, rock like substance, that takes its name from the crackling noise it makes when smoked in a pipe. It is relatively cheap and easy to buy.

It is a demon.

The addicts tell me that one hit off this stuff and a person is hooked—big time. It is so good, so in demand, that there are already turf wars developing over who is going to control its distribution in Tacoma. On the streets, people refer to the addicts as crackheads and rockstars.

One attractive woman who smokes crack came to me today. She had that bleary-eyed, manic demeanor of an addict who had not slept in days. She told me one of those pathetic stories that regularly emerges from the dark world of drugs. Even as she was relating what had happened to her, I knew where the conclusion was going. Inside myself, I did not want her to continue. It was the horror story of a woman, so desperate for yet another hit off of a crack pipe, that she was willing to perform oral sex on five strangers in an all-night session of smoking and sexing. I wanted to vomit, but hung in there, racking my brains, sorting out the available resources where she could get some help. She said that she did want help. In the end, I called one of my friends in Narcotics Anonymous, and he came down to talk to her. Eventually, she walked away into the streets, the prospects of kicking the demon more than she could handle. Help me, please, but not yet.

The street addict scratches out daily existence from one fix and one compromise to the next. Mary supported her heroin addiction by prostitution; Rafael walked around with infected arms (dirty needles), having appendages so ugly that I thought they should not belong to the human body.

What to do, what to do. We have to be both wise and compassionate. We must not be naive. Addiction is a disease that kills the body and the spirit, so, we must confront it with a no-nonsense policy: no selling, no buying, no using. We must challenge every addict if in no other way than to tell them that they are living insanity.

On the other hand, addicts are a tragic and real fact on the streets of America. Our door must always be open to them. Like so many of our guests, the addict is broken, lost, sick and disgusted with him or herself. The Church must be in the midst of them all, a flesh and blood reminder of Christ The Healer, of Christ The Hope. There has to be some human intimacy in the face of the dehumanization that drugs produce. We must reach out to these brothers and sisters and not cast them out.

Tuesday, September 15th

Two brothers were in the chapel today, blood brothers, both in their late thirties, both heading in totally different directions. Walker is an alcoholic drifter, an intelligent and very likeable man, whom I have known for years; at one time, he was a successful real estate agent in Santa Fe. Jules, his brother, is a local businessman, raising a young family in Tacoma. Walker had asked me to facilitate their meeting since it had been two years since they had seen each other.

It was one of those reunions that never makes it on TV, but it was no less poignant and full of sorrow. Jules stood there, dressed in his clean and stylish casual clothes, troubled over his brother. Walker leaned against the wall, running his hand nervously through his hair, wearing a dirty Levi jacket that gave off the residual odor of several days in a boxcar. So they talked, these two long-separated brothers. In a sense, they talked with the same abandon and warmth of the those days when they were growing up with mom and dad. That being said, Walker's slow ride into self-destruction was very present. Jules finally said to his brother, whom he clearly loved, "Come home with me, and give this all up." Painfully, a man trapped in the awful nightmare of his own making, Walker simply shook his head. No, he could not do it. In the end, whatever his love for his family, Walker's first love and last love was for his liquor.

Jules left in his new model car after thanking me and wishing his brother the best. Walker, too, thanked me, slipped on his weathered backpack and headed for the train yards. If he lives, I will probably see him next year when it is apple harvest time in Wenatchee.

Sunday, October 11th

At Mass this morning, halfway through what I considered to be a fairly decent homily, a young stranger stood up slowly in the middle of the crowd and asked, "So what's the point, Father?" I chuckled. It was funny. How many times have I wanted to stand up in a religious service and pose the same question to some well-meaning phony droning on and on and on from the pulpit. I told the guy, as we all laughed, that I was coming to the point (I guess). Be patient.

Sunday morning Mass on the streets. I struggle over what to say when I preach because this congregation has had its belly full of empty Christianity, and, too, it is a very diverse group. Nevertheless, there is a joy in knowing that the language I am using is making contact with a very critical audience.

Everything happens: people have seizures, people snore. Some of the mentally ill will make silent or muffled commentaries, their lips never stopping. One time, Skinny Lynn started frying eggs back on the kitchen stove during a moment of total silence; there was another occasion when Dutch, after receiving communion, proceeded to one of the couches and punched out Fred. People have told me to preach, "real good." Others have asked me not to preach. Still others asked me to hustle because there was an important game on TV which even God did not want to miss.

The most important truth that I try to express at these times is that of the centrality of God's love for all of us. It is a truth that has to be crafted well in the images of the streets with people who feel so obscure and abandoned. But I can never stop there. The poor understand that love without deeds is not love. We are all challenged to share God's love with one another as we live on the streets: a cup of coffee shared, a kind word spoken, an argument abandoned, patience with a disagreeable person given, a supportive hand to a sick or elderly brother or sister extended.

It is their sense of devotion that always knocks me out and lifts me up. I am privileged, from my position, to see and hear the faith of people who have endured much hardship. The prayers for various intentions include not just individual needs, but speak to the needs of the rest of the people on the streets; indeed, one woman regularly prays for "everyone in the whole world." We are, in this Skid Row Mass, a long distance from the warmth and functional architecture of most churches, and we are certainly very different from the carefully planned liturgies of a suburban parish, but the abundance of good hearts and bowed heads make this Sunday Mass a very sacred moment on the streets. It is a gift to me to be in the presence of my friends when they pray. They help me get to the point.

Monday, November 9th

Another Monday and a day off. It is such a relief for me and the staff to hit Sunday night. When I look around at my staff at the end of the day, Pat and Mary Ann, who are our two new Jesuit Volunteers, and Neil and Stacy, I see whipped faces. We feel swamped by it all: by the passing conversations of so many people (there were over 250 people in Nativity House yesterday); by people wanting more time; by strangers in need; by the glitches in preparing meals; by the constant pressure of maintaining peace and order. There has been a relentless assault on the senses; lots of noise; the smell of cigarette smoke and body odor; sights of individuals who are happy, sad, pensive, sullen, stoned, lost, fearful, excited, hungry. During the day, we have broken up a few potential fights (we are street-wise United Nations negotiators), disinfected and bound up wounds, handed out a ton of aspirin, chased off some maybe-drug dealers out in front, kissed and hugged some new babies and their new moms, done a counselor's load of telephone calls, made several trips to the clothesroom to outfit a needy person, and reached out to lots of loners.

Friday, December 18th

This has been a week of death.

Jack was shot dead on Monday, his body dumped in an intersection on the East Side. It was a dope deal that went awry. His girlfriend, Cynthia, called me from jail where she is in protective custody. She not only saw the killers, but watched them blow Jack away. "Wasted." What a tragically perfect word. What a waste; this guy had so much talent and so much potential, and it was all used in the pursuit of making the fast buck. But in the merciless world of dealing and buying drugs, there is always someone who plays the game better and more ruthlessly. That late sixties' song drifts around in my head as I work through my feelings: "Goddamn the Pusherman."

I did the graveside funeral for Maria on Wednesday. She was forty-three. Dead of complications resulting from alcoholism. It was a very moving service. Her three Blackfoot brothers had come from eastern Montana, and, accompanied by their hand drums, they chanted in their native language. Their hymn was stark and vulnerable. The ancient way with all its divine and human power neutralized the cold December wind.

Bridget was killed two days ago; she wasn't even thirty years old. Struck by a hit and run driver. The word on the streets is that she was wired on some drugs that she had slammed into her arm twenty minutes before in some shabby motel room. She probably never knew what hit her. I am sorrowful over this; not a month ago, Bridget and I talked in the jail where she was completing a six-month sentence for boosting goods at a local big name clothes outlet—to support her drug habit. She sounded so great then, so upbeat, so hopeful; she was looking foward to living a clean and clear life and to being united with her young son. Her boyfriend has been in and out of Nativity House since the whole thing happened, needing to talk.

He is lost and does not have any friends. Bridget was everything.

Sunday, December 20th

Neil and I are big Blues music fans; usually, we have a tape or two lying around to play on the Nativity House Boom Box. Many of our guests are knowledgeable about this kind of music, and probably all of them can relate to the message of the Blues. It was out of this meaning of the Blues that Neil wrote in our Christmas newsletter:

> Street people are not the only ones with the Blues. We all live the Blues and have earned the right to sing our stories. The hard part is helping others to understand the Blues we sing and understanding the songs of others. Christ, in the love that only God can have, understands everything in us, all that falls between sorrow and joy. When we respond to Christ's love, we choose to enter into a more basic emotional stream which allows us to flow into the hearts of others, to flow into their Blues. The meeting of hearts in the stream of Christ's love is where one can know healing.

> At Nativity House, we recognize the common stream which connects all: bankers and hoboes, bakers and prostitutes, homemakers and mentally ill. We all believe that common stream is God, in our midst, inviting us to reach out and share in the sufferings and joys of each other. It is as if by sharing and listening we all become the Blues singer and the understanding audience—unified at once in Christ. In that unity, we can slowly overcome the Blues.

On the streets, the joy of Christmas paradoxically includes the pain which the Blues express. Only God can make sense of suffering.

Friday, December 25th (Christmas)

We opened up before dawn this morning. It is important that no one be walking on the streets alone today. The staff was greeted at 6 AM by a host of the troops. We all pitched in to clean up from the Christmas Eve celebration, started cracking a million eggs for our gourmet breakfast, and plugged in the coffee. O, blessed are good smells and a warm place on Christmas morning.

And the first gift of the day: Ol' Mac handed me a ten dollar bill—"for all the coffee I drink here, and maybe to buy some diapers if there is a need."

❖ *1988* ❖

Little Band of Mystics

Wednesday, January 6th

Terry and Sarah asked me a year ago to officiate at their wedding. As I inform all couples, who ask me if I would marry them, I told them to see me in a year, and, if they are still together, then I would seriously consider it. Street liaisons are notoriously fast and very unstable. They might look good, but personal problems lurk beneath the surface, like hidden dynamite, and the ecstasy of romance frequently blows up. So I prefer to wait it out. In the case of Terry and Sarah, I agreed to do the honors.

They are a young couple, and, for a while last year, were on the streets until he found work in his trade as a mechanic. Sarah is a gentle woman who suffered brain damage at birth. The disability left her partially handicapped in speech and in some of her leg movements. People often think she is intoxicated when she walks and speaks. I like Sarah and Terry; I like what I see as they express their care for one another.

So the grand wedding took place in the little apartment where they lived. The apartment had been divided in half by borrowed metal chairs, simulating an aisle. When the wedding began, someone put on a tape of a song by Chicago, and Sarah made her glorious entrance from the kitchen—the half kitchen. In the front row sat her foster parents, both elderly, both deaf, both beaming. As I was asking the questions of the marriage vows, and the happy couple was responding, Sarah, her free hand behind her back, was furiously "signing" everything that was being said in order that her parents—intently watching that joyful little hand—could follow the whole ceremony. When I realized what was going on, I started to choke up.

After the formal part of the evening, we all adjourned to kitchen for all the free cake and 7-Up we could eat and drink.

It was a wedding as tender in its humanity as any in which I have been involved.

Thursday, January 16th

A close call two days ago. Tanya, whacked out on drugs and very angry that I would not lend her money to score some more dope, stormed out of Nativity House only to return with a broken bottle in hand. Destination: Me. Pat, I, and some quick-thinking guests pulled her down to the floor, but not before she had sliced my hand. At first, in the adrenalin rush of it all, I did not know that I had been cut. Then I saw the blood.

"Is that your blood, Pat?"

"Nope, Big Guy," said Pat, "It's yours."

The biggest pain in the whole episode was the long wait at the hospital to obtain a tetanus shot.

Tanya called me this afternoon from jail, very apologetic, protesting that she was under the influence. I told her that whatever excuse she had, she would have to take responsibility for her acts and therefore would be banned from Nativity House indefinitely. She is paying another price, too. Apparently, the word of what she had done had hit the women's section of the jail, so that the authorities had put her in isolation—for protection. One does not attack Nativity House Staff.

In discussing the incident with the staff, we were faced with the question of banning someone and for how long. How do you maintain order and how do you express compassion? In Tanya's case we are looking at someone who could have done much damage and, also, someone with a sadly screwed-up existence. We opted for the indefinite ban and some sign that she was taking steps to get into a drug-treatment program. But it can be a tough call, even when all the bald facts are there. We concluded our staff meeting by joining hands and praying for the wisdom of a tough and compassionate love; it was the prayer of the Church seeking light in the darkness.

Sunday, January 18th

What a joy to see Bethany Presbyterian Church roll in with their Sunday lunch serving crew. It is a small church, but the entire congregation gets involved in providing the goodies, and now, with years of experience at Nativity House, they are at ease as they serve our guests. There is a grace in hot, steaming, nutritious stew prepared from scratch by loving and cheerful hands. Not only does it fill hungry stomachs, but it puts our huge Sunday crowd at ease, not to mention the staff. What Bethany does is repeated, in their own way, by Prince of Peace Lutheran Church and the many groups and individuals who contribute to the feeding of the homeless.

The 50 volunteers who help Nativity House from all religious persuasions have taught me, concretely, a deeper understanding of the Body of Christ. Each part of the Body can be concerned for all the other parts; and if one part is hurting, then all parts are hurting; our gifts are for the care and consolation of the entire community. The faith of these people is no fad or sentiment to be discussed casually over a nice bottle of Chardonnay; it is a reality that drives them; they want to share with and serve the poor because the poor are their brothers and sisters. They know well what is said in the Letter of James that if our faith does not lead to action, then it remains dead as a doornail. There is nothing dead about the volunteers who come to Nativity House.

Beyond what is given to our guests, in turn our guests give back. Directly, there are gifts of simple thanks and the instruction in how to be dignified and human in spite of their poverty. Indirectly, our guests show the way to the consciousness of the greater social issues of America which focus around the poor, the humiliated, the marginal.

Wednesday, February 4th

A joyful surprise today as Don walked in. He was carrying a twenty-five pound bag of sugar under his arm to donate to Nativity House. He passed on the good news of being off drugs for 25 months and—get this—he handed me his business card: he is selling cars in north Seattle. A business card? From Don? Can you believe it?

"Just wanted to come in and say hi and say thanks and, by the way, Father," he said with his big grin and shining dark eyes, "if you want a good deal on a car, give me a call."

As we visited and he filled me in on the road to freedom, I recalled the broken man of two years ago, beaten, lost, and his arms so full of needle scars and collapsed veins that they looked liked he had suffered from a terrible shotgun blast or some prodigious form of mutant arm-smallpox. With tears in his eyes, he expressed his gratitude for the patience and help that the staff at Nativity House had given him.

I thank God tonight for the healing of Don, for giving us the ability to choose. I wonder, too, if God ever "feels" like this whole human enterprise is a risk that should not have been taken, given the consummate mess into which we can hurl ourselves. I am thinking here especially of the obsession for drugs which can reduce us to such pitiful states. I am consoled by the lines in the book of Wisdom as I watch Don, in my mind's eye, strolling out the door:

> Yes, you love all that exists,
>> you hold nothing you have made in abhorrence,
> for had you hated anything
>> you would not have formed it.
> You spare all things
> because all things are yours, Lord, Lover of life,
>> you whose imperishable spirit is in all. (Ws. 11:24-27)

Tuesday, March 2nd

Two prostitutes recently had babies. Alice brought her baby in; he had a red face and looked so damn little. The tiny guy was passed round from cooing person to cooing person and even Barney—frown-faced Barney—gave his half-smile approval. I always have mixed emotions in this kind of a situation: happy that there is life and not death, but sad because I know that Child Protective Services (CPS) is watching the situation very carefully. CPS may separate the mother and child—for the sake of both.

In one of those it-could-only-happen-at-Nativity-House moments, we received a call from Barbara, who has a variety of "regular customers."

She had called from the labor room of the hospital and proceeded to give the staff a play-by-play description of her contractions. The baby was born two hours later, and that evening, after we closed up, Stacy, Neil, and I went down for a visit. On arriving, we checked out the little one, there in a glassed-in room for the newborn, learning that CPS had already taken the baby from Barbara because of her cocaine addiction. Of course, the child was born an addict. Already it was going through the symptoms of drug withdrawal: muscular agitation, some spasms, and border-line seizures. We went on to see Barbara who was walking around in her room, pushing her IV stand in front of her, smoking a cigarette. She was not full of the joy of a mother, but full of guilt and that manic behavior of an addict who is into forced withdrawal. Even though we may well have been her only family, at that moment I wanted to shake her. The whole thing was madness.

Tuesday, March 15th

Maureen called me today. She is multi-talented and uses most of her time and energies in service of the poor. Today, she was up to her neck in the search for affordable housing for a poor family. Later on, Marty and Dave wandered in, taking a break from their work with drug addicts. Even the most bitter addict has nothing but praise for these two guys. At lunch time, Vince, from the Health Department's Crisis Team arrived to help us talk with a mentally ill guest. Now, there is a man who does have the patience of Job. This afternoon I had coffee with Lonnie, a two-term Special Forces Nam Vet who hunts for and helps some of the lost street brothers damaged by the war.

Where is the Spirit of God in the urban scene? Surely, God walks and loves in the dedication of those people who give their time and hearts for the rights and care of the poor. They are a legion: public nurses, shelter providers, housing advocates, men-

tal health care workers, church folks who prowl the midnight
bars offering a sympathetic ear, free meal providers, AA and NA
meeting leaders, senior care personnel, drug rehab counselors
working overtime, gentle paramedics, caring police officers,
those who assist the physically and developmentally handicapped, always-available clergy men and women, Vietnam Out-
reach. I cannot name them all, but I have seen them all on the
grateful faces of the poor whom they serve.

These good people are signs of hope in the city. They are
constantly giving birth to God's Spirit.

Friday, April 1st

Jolie finally talked with me recently. She is an extraordinar-
ily beautiful, green-eyed prostitute, a drug addict, and a college
graduate. I have had this hunch for weeks that she wanted to
talk, but she has always avoided me whenever I initiated a conversation. One day, looking drawn and malnourished, she asked
if she could get some clothes, and there, in the clothesroom,
away from the peering eyes of the crowd, she spilled her pain.

There have been, subsequently, several clothesroom talks.
It is difficult for me and for her, because there is a kind of tenderness and love which exists between us in the eye of her terrible storm. Neither wants to hurt the other. I dislike confronting
her with her manner of self-degradation and self-destruction;
she, for her part, dislikes confronting me with the truth of her
prostitution, her addiction, and her unwillingess to change her
behavior, in spite of her acknowledged pain.

I am attracted to her, to her intelligence, to her inner
beauty. More than anything else, I want her to be whole.

Monday, April 18th

Some of the most gifted of our guests are prostitutes. We
have come to know them in their tears and fears and hopes. We

emotionally travel with them as they walk the streets, as they battle their addictions, when they do time in jail. We visit them in hospitals after some crazy customer has beaten them up; occasionally we bury them.

Why does someone become a prostitute? As I ponder that tonight, I know there is no simple answer; it is very complex. Frequently, it can be attributed to childhood sexual abuse, parental abandonment, neglect, rejection, lack of love. It is a life built upon one pathetic insecurity and dehumanization after another. The subsequent use of drugs, often connected with prostitution, is a way to obliterate the pain of life. Prostitution is an acting out of the hatred of self and the hatred of those who abuse.

This whole damn business is fueled by those twin merchants of death: men who see women as objects, chunks of pleasurable meat, and, secondly, by a culture which often exploits the female body to sell its products. On the basis of the sick and gory stuff that I see on the streets, it is clear to me that prostitution is never a case of someone just having a good time for a few bucks; it is always a case of some kind of death-dealing.

Sometimes, Nativity House is criticized because it has prostitutes on the premises. These women are, after all, frequently addicts, often with police records, and often have done time in jail. Such criticisms were leveled at Christ. He was with sinners (often that meant prostitutes) and the tax collectors (the real creeps of the time), and he was with them because they needed his care and not necessarily the we-have-it-together people. "It is not the healthy who need the doctor, but the sick." (Mk. 2:17) Nativity House, indeed the Church, can do no less. The women of the streets who are prostitutes—for whatever reason—need our compassion and care and truth. They know we disagree with what they do; they know we will gently challenge them. They know, too, that we will be there for them and love them unconditionally; they know that we long for their healing and wholeness and happinesss, which, deep down, they all desire for themselves. They desire it because that is the way God made them. It seems to me this is our most sacred task at Nativity House: to help all find their way to the truth of God's creative love.

Friday, April 29th

The drug trafficking on Commerce Street is becoming a
major headache. It is like a pharmacy out there; one can acquire
any drug desired. I am sure that the Tacoma Police Department
is video-taping all the activity, and, as soon as any one of the
participants comes into Nativity House, we will be accused of
being a party to the whole business, even if a naive party. It
gripes me. Why aren't the police on the street, up front, making
their presence known? Drug dealers disappear when the cops
are around. I can manage the situation inside Nativity House,
but I cannot control what goes on outside. I will be the first to
celebrate the absence of drug dealing on Commerce Street.

Saturday, May 7th

As a wrung-out staff was leaving this Saturday night, we
ran into a wild situation. I opened the door and was face to face
with Ron, a burly Vietnam vet, who refers to himself as "God."
In his disturbed way, he really believes this, especially when he
has been drinking. He stood there, staring at me, blood pouring
down his face. He had been fighting with several people. I was
looking into a very crazed face, and I thought for a split second,
my heart pounding away, that he was going to clobber me with a
large chunk of cement he was holding. As quickly as he was
there, he turned and ran into the middle of the street and flung
the cement at a crowd of perceived antagonists who were waiting on the other side of the street. It was war. We called the
police and paramedics immediately as Ron started to slug it out
with all comers. When they arrived—in record time—it took
four cops to restrain him.

It was bedlam: a hot afternoon, agitated people milling
around, several squad cars, nervous paramedics, Ron lying in the
middle of a downtown street, hands cuffed behind his back, his
blood splattered from one side of the street to the other. We
stood there, stunned.

But wait a minute. Around the corner, in the midst of all the chaos, behold, here comes manic-depressive Stephen, now manic as hell, a bunch of wildflowers in his hand, and singing/shouting—at the top of his lungs—for the whole universe to hear. He was singing the National Anthem.

He came trudging down the street, this little troubadour, flowers in hand, and, suddenly, everyone stopped: the cops struggling with Ron, Ron struggling with the cops, the crowd of street people, a bewildered and what-should-we-do-now Nativity House Staff, curious passers-by. All eyes were on Stephen. He kept on coming, moving through another, "O Say Can You See." He then stopped at our front door and handed me the flowers: "For you, Pastor Gary." With that, he merrily hummed his way down Commerce Street, heading, I presume, for home. I don't think he was aware of anything other than the exhilaration of singing "The Star Spangled Banner" and in making the flower delivery to Nativity House.

We hung around for a few minutes more, ensuring that Ron was taken off safely to the hospital.

When I arrived home, my Jesuit housemate, Pat, asked, "How was your day? Do want a beer?"

"Make it scotch on the rocks, Pat, and I am going to tell you a story that you won't believe."

Thursday, May 26th

The City of Tacoma is threatening to close Nativity House. They are going after any facility that has some connection with the rapidly expanding drug business. Since we are in that downtown area where there is intensive drug activity, and since many street people are addicts, it figures that they would target us. The mayor was even on TV referring to us as, "That drug den." It was a cheap shot. This is the same mayor who has refused countless invitations to have lunch with our guests. I know no one is selling, buying, or using drugs within Nativity House, but why not visit and see for yourself, Mr. Mayor?

There is another factor in the whole scenario. The local business community has never been happy with the street population, not to mention a place like Nativity House. From the sound of some of their letters and public remarks, I think they are very anxious to see us closed down.

Friday, May 27th

The fight is on with the City and the City Attorney's Office. When I was community organizing in Oakland, we described this kind of situation as one of power against power. I know the game. And if the city wants it, they will get it. I am hurt and I am mad, but I know we hold the factual and moral high ground.

Our strategy has to be pressure, lots of political and moral pressure. The City Attorney has sent us a three page letter which basically says that they are going to close us down. I leaked it to the Tacoma press. I called fifty church, business and political leaders in the Tacoma area whom I knew to be sympathetic to Nativity House. Our Board Chairperson and I contacted a tough, top-notch civil rights lawyer. Our Board of Directors was systematically briefed on what was happening, and together they worked out a straight-ahead, here-are-the-facts strategy.

I made an announcement to all of the street people at a packed house that we were all in this together, and it was their fight, too. I broke down and wept during that announcement. I choked-up again when several of our guests came to me asking for paper and pencil to write a letter to the City Attorney and the local newspaper. How much I love this place and the people we serve!

Monday, May 30th

The city attorney's office is being overwhelmed with letters and phone calls. The same is true for the mayor's office and that of the chief of police. The *Tacoma News Tribune* is printing some very supportive letters. A delegation of our Board and our lawyer is meeting with the Mayor, Police Chief, and City Attorney. My sense is that the city is a bit bewildered and surprised at our community support.

Wednesday, June 1st

The distraction of this fight with the City has made it difficult to be present to our guests, but they are constantly making an effort to be present to me. One drug dealer came in and explained to me why the streets were vacant outside. He said, "We have been trying to run everybody off, Father, out of respect for what Nativity House does for all the people down here." It was working; the streets were deserted. Another young man, one of our guests, gave me a copy of a three-page letter which he had meticulously typed at the library and personally presented to what must have been an astonished City Attorney. Here are a few of his words:

> So what do we less fortunates do now that you are trying to close one of our sanctuaries? Do you corral us and rail us out of town? Or gas us? Or ignore us? Or do you try dealing with us? A society is judged as to how they treat the poorest classes. Nativity House is a dream turned reality, a safety net for the thousands whom have passed its way. We are people who needed nourishment—of mind and body. And we got it there. Perhaps some of us will go out and help others overcome their struggles.

> Closing Nativity House under the heading of being an alleged drug den is an act of sheer desperation by a society that is simply missing the problem. The problem, dear City of Tacoma, is a fucked-up society; the problem is drugs on the streets, not in the Nativity House.

Friday, June 3rd

Today, five of our Board members and our lawyer met with the Mayor, Chief of Police, and the City Attorney. The City is backing away from their threats and calling off the hunt. I am sure that the public pressure—especially from the Church community—and the City's growing awareness of what we do on the streets are contributing factors. The meeting ended amicably. Some steps are to be taken including a higher police presence in the area. We may assist by hiring some off duty police officers to patrol the front of Nativity House, but only on a temporary basis. Money is tough enough without forking out twenty bucks an hour to pay for a job that is not ours to do.

I stayed away from any contact or meetings with the City, preferring to let the Board do the point work; after all they are the ones who must take the flack and who are ultimately responsible for the policies and actions of Nativity House.

I have been angry about this whole matter. I feel Nativity House has been betrayed. For years, we have cared for some of Tacoma's most unfortunate citizens, and now the City is dealing with us as if we were some kind of dangerous predator lurking on the streets. It is so hypocritical.

Sunday, June 5th

I am proud of the Board of Directors. They moved to confront these recent charges with speed and conviction. They have always been motivated by the welfare of the people of the streets, even though, given their own personal and professional responsibilities, they cannot be on the day-to-day scene. And they have been unhesitating in their support of me and the staff as we have formulated and implemented drug policies.

The unsaid story here, of course, is not that the Board was simply trying to keep open the doors of some obscure drop-in center for some obscure people. In their guts, they knew that when an all-knowing institution comes after those people, the Church has to fight. It is a very urgent fight for very specific human beings, and I do not think that a government, be it local, state or federal, can ever understand this. I am not sure it even wants to understand. The government frequently has more important agendas than looking out for the poor.

Monday, June 6th

The *Tacoma News Tribune* carried an editorial today, which not only praised the City for backing off, but also gave us much support for our program. We are over the hump.

We have made it, thanks to many people from the larger community.

Thursday, June 30th

There is a tall, thin, aging poet on the scene. Claude carries a plastic bag for his clothes and a tattered briefcase for his poetry. He wears an oversized football helmet which makes him look pretty ridiculous. It turns out that he wears the helmet to protect himself when he has seizures.

To talk with him is a delight. He has lots of stories and has traveled quite a bit, living off the land, meeting many people and having many experiences. He writes continually and periodically uses a library typewriter to make good copies of his poetry. Here is an excerpt from a poem written after a Church service at Nativity House:

Now many guests attending a service
Are bringing tough problems along too,
   But please set them at ease
   Showing exactly how God helped you.

Tuesday, June 5th

Kenny died in my arms yesterday. He had been at the hospital in the last round with cirrhosis of the liver. A few hours before, when I had stepped out of his room, we went through his final ritual of care.

"Father Gary, two words."

"What's that, Kenny?"

"Love you."

He was thirty-seven, a great sensitive soul, and I shall be proud and honored to be doing his funeral in a few days. This death was very hard for me. Ken was one of the first people I met on the streets of Tacoma, and his was a friendship I always cherished. And if I cared for this man so much, how much more the God who made both of us.

Friday, July 15th

A middle-aged mother came in recently, looking for her teenage daughter. The searching face of a parent we have seen many times.

I remember a New York cab driver once telling me, as he pointed to a crumbled, passed-out old man on the sidewalk, "You know, that guy had a mother once." Again I think of a 75-year-old matriarch whom I knew in the neighborhoods of Oakland when I was a community organizer. Lucille was grieving over her mentally distressed daughter. She said: "O, Gary, you never stop being a momma." I recall, too, my own mother sending me a couple of bucks a month, when I was a struggling student at San Jose State.

Tonight, I ponder a long series of mommas. The mother of a young addict came in and handed me a check for Nativity House, informing me that she had been saving money for the inevitable funeral of her daughter, but felt that we could use it for our work. As we stood there, I flashed on a California mother, photograph of her missing daughter in hand. She had traveled from shelter to shelter, up and down the West Coast:

Did we know her daughter? Had we seen her? Could we suggest where she might continue her search?

One mother, nearly at the end of her emotional rope, found her mentally ill son sitting in the back of Nativity House and begged him to return to the treatment that he had been undergoing. No luck. He simply ignored her. Another woman confronted her disaffected daughter and the daughter's boyfriend during one of our lunches. There was lots of yelling and screaming and tears, and more frustration. Then Phillip's mom called me from Detroit; she knew of me because of her boy's letters. Had I seen him? Is he okay? Phillip was there, and I put him on the phone. There was a big grin on his face. A few months later, we received a check from a mother in Iowa, sent in memory of her son, killed in an Arizona railroad town. He had spoken to her often of his home away from home: Nativity House.

We are a bridge that extends from the streets to the hearts of relatives, who, for known and unknown reasons, have sons and daughters on the streets of America. We try to connect them if we can. Lucille was right: You never stop being a momma.

Friday, September 2nd

I was called to the hospital last night. Ben had been taken there after suffering a stroke and falling on his head. He had been drinking very heavily. I think he is 28 years old. He was on a respirator and the prognosis was poor.

When I entered the waiting room, there were a half-dozen street folks there, a straggly group of Ben's friends. I could tell that their unkempt appearance and loud and unremitting grieving was annoying the hospital staff. That was understandable. What Ben's friends really wanted was a chance to see him, and I convinced the duty nurse to let me take them in, one at a time, to see their buddy. After all, they might not see him alive again.

Ben was unconscious, and the room was full of the sounds of monitoring machines, the respirator, and suction apparatus. How tender and moving to see each individual gently touch and talk with Ben. Undaunted, each sang his song of loyalty and care.

It was the kind of truth-telling which rose above the depressing noises and smells.

After all had paid their respects, one of the six suggested that we pray for Ben. With the help of one of the nurses, we adjourned to a nearby room. The nurse, taken by the remarkable show of raw love and devotion, asked to join us, and there, at 1 AM, I heard some of the most honest prayer of my life, powered by the importance of friendship and the recognition that God, ultimately, "calls the shots." We stood, hand in hand, and finished with the the Lord's Prayer.

Where are the mystics of this world? In monasteries? In pulpits? In mountain caves? In boxcars? In garbage dumps? Who knows? Wherever they are, they are to be found in that place where God meets and loves human beings profoundly and moves them to love their human family. In those moments in that hushed hospital room, I felt I was with my own little band of mystics.

We learned earlier today that Ben is improving, although it looks like he'll be paralyzed on one side. He is a man of great intelligence, but that intelligence has been sleeping. It is strange, but maybe the stroke will wake it up.

Wednesday, September 15th

We are seeing more and more Mexican and Central American nationals making their way up the West Coast from homes that stretch from Panama to the North of Mexico. They are strangers in this land. When work is not available, they will wind up—at least for a few days—at Nativity House. I am grateful to have Mary Ann on my staff; besides being a caring and sensitive person, she is also fluent in Spanish. How many times I have seen the eyes of one of our guests light up when she speaks in their native tongue.

Theirs is a different kind of fear here on the streets, these Hispanic brother and sisters. Without access to English, the most basic things become a major problem: where can they get medical help, how to find a job, how to use a bus, where can one sleep? In addition, they live in the constant fear of the Immigration and Naturalization Service (INS), which can swoop down and pack them back across the border. There is also the fear born of the prejudice directed toward them, simply because they are of color and do not speak English.

Our policy is clear, whether they are documented or undocumented: They are hungry and we feed them; they are thirsty and we give them something to drink; they are strangers and we make them welcome.

Thursday, September 29th

A close friend of mine, someone who has worked on the streets, has been raped. I am sick and full of rage. I was with her the morning after it all happened. Holding her in my arms fell so short of the grief and fury I felt. In moments like this, I feel like cutting off half the penises of the world.

How can such a terrible thing happen to such a good person? Rape. Even the word looks and sounds ugly, barren, and empty. How can God allow this? How can God endure the calculated evil of the rapist? What can I do? No theology of the ultimate justice of God means anything to me right now. I want justice immediately and all the pain that my friend will endure to be taken away.

I want this man punished.

Saturday, October 1st

Some street people know of the rape. One individual came to me, someone I had never met, and told me that the word was out that a friend of many street people and of mine had been raped. This guy, who seemed to be well connected, said that street people are listening. He then told me that if the man who hurt my friend starts blabbing and bragging, he is dead meat. I said to him that I would prefer—and so would she—that any information which would help to catch the rapist should be turned over to the police.

He responded to my words with a slight head shake and said, "No disrespect toward you, Father, but that isn't the way it goes down with us."

Tuesday, October 11th

We had an old adage in the community organizing world (at least I did): go in their door, and come out your own. It sounds suspiciously like the kind of thing one would expect of a sneaky and conniving Jesuit, but when it comes to raising money, one does have to endure much in order to get to the goal.

In the early evening yesterday, I went to a fraternity of a local university. They had requested some thoughts on homelessness and informed me that the fraternity would make a small donation. I was greeted at the door by someone who looked at me like: who are you, Mr. Gray Hair with the crummy windbreaker? I responded with who I was, whereupon the president of the fraternity came in and greeted me, "Father Brown, how are you?" I told him that I was Father Smith. Later I got only five minutes before dinner, and then I was introduced as Father Kelly. Again I said that I was Father Smith (I'm English, not Irish). I spoke about the fact that people were going through Safeway dumpsters less than a mile from the University, and related a few facts regarding the contrast between the haves and the have-nots in our culture.

On the spot, they voted to contribute a check to Nativity House for $500. And then, they excused me.

I left happy, sent on my gray-haired way by the same fellow who greeted me. As I left he said, "Thanks for coming, Father Jones." I didn't bother correcting for a third time. I knew who I was.

I chuckled all the way to the car, the five hundred Big Ones in my pocket. O, the humiliations that a Director must tolerate to keep food on the table.

Saturday, October 15th

One of those nonstop days. Our new staffers, Carol and Bill, along with the vets, Pat, Mary Ann, and myself, were hopping. A series of images: Colby, trying to be casual as he told me he had AIDS; Wayne defecating in his pants and not knowing it; an angry pimp coming in looking for "his woman," and me telling him to leave; Fay's face breaking out from a batch of dirty cocaine; Art weeping in the office over the loss of his baby son (born with too many physical complications); a local businessman who is being harrassed asking for help; Douglas's father dying in Los Angeles—could we help him patch together busfare so he can make the funeral? We can; fixing the plumbing underneath the kitchen sink which had ripped loose, spilling water everywhere; chatting with the new and likeable beat cops; Carol spending hours tracking down a temporary residence for a young family which has just hit town; Lesley, a transvestite agitated over life in general, and wanting to talk; Pat, using his best negotiating skills, settling down two people who have been verbally sniping at each other for a week; Mary Ann, directing and organizing several instant volunteers to move a huge load of food upstairs.

As we are relaxing at at the end of the day, Popeye came in to tell us, "You guys are the greatest."

A busy day. A good day. Thanks, Popeye.

Wednesday, October 26th

Word reached me today that a former Jesuit classmate has hanged himself. He was apparently doing well in his work in the Southwest. What happened? Was there some kind of psychotic episode induced by medication? Did he just plain out crack? Was there just too much stress, too much pressure? Did he try to do too much alone? Were there support people in his busy life?

What keeps me going? How do I take care of myself in a street ministry full of strain and tension? Where is my nourishment? When I scratch away at those questions, I know that the answers always have human faces. I could not keep going were it not for my friends, for the support they give me. It is in the relationships I have with wonderful people where I have discovered my capacities for growth and change and enduring love. And there are a few men and women whose manner of loving me and cherishing me has made the difference in those dark moments we all have. When I think of these people, how I love them and how they love me, the line from Herman Hesse's *Narcissus and Goldmund* inevitably comes to mind: "It is thanks to you that my heart has not dried up, that a place within me has remained open to grace."

Of course, I believe that I am sustained, too, by God's grace. But I have only come to know God's presence and God's pursuit through other human beings. And this truth is the engine that drives my passion to reach out to the people of the streets. How on earth can they believe in a loving God, in a compassionate God, in a righteous God, in a God of the poor and abandoned unless they experience these qualities in another human being? If we do not have the experience of human love in our lives, then I think all the preaching in the world about God's love is just pie in the sky.

I am grateful, O God, for those friends whom, ultimately, in your Providence, you have given to me. Without them, I am a shell. With them, I am becoming more of the human being that you want me to be: good and holy and truthful and just, and one who bears, in some small way, your forgiving and compassionate love to those who otherwise would not know it.

Sunday, November 20th

We have been in the midst of some brutally cold weather. The clothesroom is getting cleaned out as people stay warm with lots of clothing. Rosco is this delicate fellow who must hold the world's record for layers of clothing. Today, he decided to get a complete change of wardrobe. As we chatted away in the clothesroom, he proceeded to remove each item in the following order: a huge filthy parka, a corduroy jacket, a flimsy wind-breaker, an old green wool sweater, a shot-full-of-holes black sweatshirt, a what-used-to-be-long-sleeved Arrow dress shirt (the pocket crammed full of pens and pencils), a white short-sleeved shirt, two T-shirts, and the tops to some long underwear. In addition, he had on two pairs of pants, a pair of shorts, and the bottoms to the long underwear. I tried to be nonchalant as the little guy was peeling off this mountain of clothing, but it was astonishing. I was able to replace just about everything, but the parka, and, of course he kept the pens and pencils.

Staff always has to be alert at this time of year and in this kind of weather for anyone doing excessive scratching—a sure sign of lice. With an abundance of clothing and the unwillingness on the part of some to take showers, there exist the conditions for lice. They have a field day next to those heavily wrapped up and toasty bodies.

Thursday, December 15th

There are a lot of ways to love somebody, but one of the most difficult is when it takes the form of hard-nosed, in-your-face confrontation.

Ralph is a lanky drifter, in and out of Nativity House over time. He spent a few years in the army, a few years in jail, and a lot of years drinking. On occasion, he has used heroin. He is a loveable young man and has a great loyalty and love for me.

Today, I challenged him on his alcoholism. I had this hunch that it was time to hit him hard and that he trusted me enough for me get away with it. I threw the madness and self-destruction of his life back in his face. It was a conversation that was like a fight, lasting for hours, moving from one end of Nativity House to the other with Ralph reeling, bobbing, and weaving. At one point, we wound up on the stairs leading to the storage room, then into the storage room, then outside and around the block, then into a coffee shop, finally back to Nativity House.

"When are you going to stop kidding yourself, Ralph? When are you going to stop lying to yourself and hating yourself? When are you going to face the fact that you are going nowhere and constantly denying that you want to go somewhere? Do you know what a collosal jerk you are when you are on the sauce? Do you want to wind up a fifty-year-old pickle brain who has no friends, no home, no hope, no life?"

Ralph fought and backed off, wept and sighed, paced with animation and sat with lean shoulders bent over; he looked at me and looked away; he followed me around and shouted at me from a distance. It was a very sustained and painful conversation for both of us. He means very much to me—and I to him.

I wish I could say tonight, as I sit here writing, that Ralph has turned the corner. I simply don't know. This disease is so cunning. In its power people are capable of rationalizing the most obvious acts of self-deception. But he will always know that I loved him enough to challenge him with the truth. He will always know that I long for him to make the choices that will mean sanity and peace. And when he is ready, I will be there to support him.

Wednesday, December 21st

Pat was sharing with the staff his frustration over the recent elections and their lack of immediacy to the problems of our society. He has been spending lots of time of late with a young woman guest and her baby. She has problems with spouse abuse, problems with the acquisition of food and diapers, problems locating sufficient funds to pay gas and light bills. The whole thing takes on that much more poignancy when one considers it is the Christmas season. All, in fact, is not calm and bright. Pat wrote this recently:

> During a debate George Bush mentioned "one thousand points of light." I wonder if he would consider Nativity House as one of those points? Is there a light, perhaps a star, which shines on Commerce Street? If so the light might catch the tear-streaked face of Kim and that of her frightened son. It is the spirit of the birth of Jesus in our midst that we celebrate at Christmas. I believe that spirit

lives in Kim, who prays daily for the strength to perse-
vere, despite the burden of an abusive mate and uncaring
bureaucracies and an uncertain future.

❖ *1989* ❖

Bearing His Wounded
Companion

Sunday, January 15th

Here is one of those head-shaking contrasts that exists in America: half of the country was sitting at home tonight, whooping it up over the Super Bowl, and on a poorly-lit narrow street—a few blocks from skid row—I dropped off little Cathy at her seedy apartment. She is a heroin addict, wasting away, separated from family, children, and, I guess you could say, separated from herself. I have these images going through my mind of the two worlds: steamy locker room interviews with the conquering gladiators and the biting cold of that alley; lots of flowing champagne and her empty refrigerator; promise of the next victorious football season and no hope—zippo—for the next day.

I am not blaming anybody, but something is sick and wrong.

Wednesday, February 22nd

Bob and Francine were ushered into our chapel where I heard a story of courage and love. He was dying of cancer at the age of forty and was receiving treatment at a local VA hospital. She had come out from the midwest to be with him, bringing along their three children who were staying with friends in Seattle. They were very educated people, very genuine, and needed some help. Could I assist them with some money? I took some money from our little slush fund and gave it to them. They saw it as a loan and would pay me back when they could.

That night one of my Jesuit housemates told me a sad story about a couple who came to his church and were in tough times. They asked him if it would be possible to obtain a small loan. The man was dying of cancer, and she had come all the way from Michigan to be with him, leaving their children in the midwest with her mother.

I looked up from the salad that I was eating, head cocked, and asked, "Were they a young couple?"

"Well, yes, as a matter of fact, they were," he responded.

I inquired, "Did he say he was a vet?"

"Yes, he did."

I probed further, "Was she wearing a smart suit, and was he wearing a turtleneck sweater?"

My housemate, sensing that look in my eyes, said, "Yeah, that's right, they were. Did you meet them, Gary?"

I sure had met them.

I called around to a variety of church contacts. Before these folks left town that day, they had hit about twenty different churches, and were successful. There was no record of this guy ever being at the VA. They made a good haul in one day's work. So much for the experienced nose of Mr. Street-wise.

I consider this to be the worst kind of scam. It is taking money and food from the poor who have so little anyway.

Thursday, March 16th

When I see a drug addict in recovery, all the discouragement and bitter-tasting frustration connected with the drug culture eases up on me. There is a change inside of me. I go from shutting down my feelings in the presence of a very sick addict (the concentration is on the practical steps necessary to get them help—if they want it) to the experience of opening up, full of joy, in the presence of someone getting healthy. There is a great happiness in witnessing a person who has kicked the shit. Darnell walked in, beaming, nine months off that monster, crack; he was bright-eyed, direct, aware. Dead and now alive. Lost and now found. We talked about the Greyhound to Houston, the trip home to the place where his dad was buried a year ago. I always told him that he needed to return someday, kneel before his dad's gravestone—and his dad's spirit—and say good-bye with dignity. And when that moment came, we would help him hustle up the money. It was time. He was ready. Darnell was poised for a longer trip than the one back to Texas.

Jolie, dear Jolie, suddenly strolled through the doors. She had stopped using drugs and had entered a rehabilitation program. She had been clean for four months. For me, given how far she was out on the edge of life, it was like four centuries.

Her decision was a day-to-day proposition, but very intentional. She had lost that scrawny look; there was actually some fat on those bones. "Fat and proud of it," she announced.

She had come in to tell me that she was okay and thanks.

There are few joys on the streets that can compare with holding a Jolie and a Darnell in my arms, feeling their beating heart against my beating heart, and knowing that they have claimed their lives and that somewhere, in that tortured road to freedom, I was a bridge. Even more, my joy flows from the knowledge that the God's love will not be denied. Ezekiel:

You were exposed in the open fields;
you were as unloved as that day you were born.
And I saw you struggling in your blood as I was passing,
and I said to you as you lay in your blood:
Live, and grow like the grass of the fields. (Ez.16:5-7)

Monday, April 3rd

I did the funeral service for little Meaghan today, dead at one month because of congenital problems. Her mother, someone I have known for a long time, was brought from jail to attend the service. I never try to make sense of these funerals, because there is simply too much that is senseless and irretrievable. I strive to be as present as possible with all the participants. Pious words just don't cut it, but friendship and care and standing with someone in their grief does.

At the end of the brief service, the mother came forward and asked to pick up her daughter. The funeral assistants gently placed Meaghan in the arms of her 18-year-old mom, and, for a moment, everyone was at peace.

Saturday, April 15th

My God, Tony was killed today, up on 15th Street, gunned down with six bullets. Those who know about these things long before the police know told me that he had sold a customer some bad dope. He had done it before. He will never do it again. I saw him only three weeks ago in the hospital where he was recuperating from a drive-by shooting. He had been hit in the leg. Tony was always living on the edge—stupidly—but there were moments in the hospital when he wept over his fear, and in gratitude that he was alive, and he promised himself that he was going to shape up. He didn't.

His broad smile was contagious. He was always friendly in Nativity House; however, on the streets he had a lethal and fast tongue and tried to be a Mr. Tough Guy. But in a drug world of Mr. Tough Guys, he was just a fish in the pond. I contacted his family in New Jersey.

Tony. Dead at twenty-four.

Friday, May 5th

Coffee. The Sacrament of the Natural Order. The icebreaker between strangers. The necessary ingredient for a long talk with a friend. The companion.

I always swore that I would never buy coffee for Nativity House. After all, people may forget to give us money and clothes and hot cereal, but they never forget to donate coffee. Therefore, the last line of defense in my trust that God will provide for us is both the presence of extra coffee upstairs, and my refusal to buy it, no matter how close we are to coffee bankruptcy.

But we were running out. And so I did the unthinkable: I bought fifteen pounds. My staff, in mock horror, saw their faith slipping away, the last fingers in the dike of belief being extracted. Mr. Trust Himself, right before their eyes, was crashing and burning. Can Earthquakes, Wars and Pestilence be far behind?

As I was triumphantly and sheepishly taking out the first pot of coffee the next day, a woman came in and said—as I was standing there holding that pot of atheistic coffee—"Can you guys use some coffee? I have some Starbucks." Starbucks? We are talking Rolls Royce of the coffee world.

I told her that we could use it, thinking we could mix the two-pound bag with the next batch of our Providence-Buster coffee. As she turned, heading for her car, she said, "I'll need some help. I have 320 pounds of it."

I didn't know whether to laugh or cry in the face of this woman who had apparently obtained the coffee legitimately A local mill needed to unload some extra supplies, and that is how she came up with it.

We have now the best free coffee west of Chicago. No question. No kidding. No contest. Maybe this will get the mayor down for a visit.

Saturday, June 3

Coming to the streets early this morning, I discovered some blood stains on the sidewalk and chalk marks that had outlined a body. On asking around and in talking with the police, it turned out that there had been a stabbing the night before, but it was not a fatal assault. The outline of that body stuck in my mind all day, a kind of metaphor for the many addicts I spoke with today. They were dead, but alive; there, but not really there.

Early in the day, I had long talks with Ted and Victor, both men who are musicians. Ted has been using heroin since his early New York days, 21 years before, and Victor hooked himself on morphine to the point of being kicked out of his Blues band. Next, I spent time with Maria and her sister, attractive people who are using drugs, wanting to quit, but not wanting to quit. Later, Roxanne told me this long story of coming down from Alaska with lots of money from the fishing business, and blowing it all on a smooth-talking gigolo and crack. At some juncture in the busy day, I discussed things with Roosevelt as he tried to cope with a dismissal from a drug treatment program. Finally, James called from jail. He had been busted the night before for possession.

I wonder how deep and wide this drug epidemic can go in America? Is there a point of no return?

Wednesday, June 28th

Bob DeLorenzo died yesterday. Cancer. He was on the Board of Directors since the early days of Nativity House. Bob was the consummate good steward, always giving and sharing his life and talents unselfishly.

He was a family man, but his family also included his friends and the poor. Few on the streets knew him, the successful businessman that he was, but the thousands who have come to Nativity House over the years never had a better friend. He quietly worked behind the scenes to ensure that there was always food on the table, and always heat in the building. He cared for my staff, for me, as if we were his own sons and daughters.

I remember Monroe's words of a few years back when I complemented him on his fine singing at a Good Friday Service: "Well, Father, I was just tryin to back ya, just tryin to back ya." That was Bob, a man who was always trying to back Nativity House with his hands and heart.

Saturday, July 1st

Watching my staff person, Mary Ann, sort out a problem with a guest in a corner today, I recalled something she had written in a newsletter about the importance of relationships.

The people of the streets are constantly calling us back to the reality of our interconnectedness. In the times of despair and fear, there is always a brother or sister willing to welcome us back. They remind us that we are bound in such a way that we can let go of our restricted view of the world, and we can open up to the possibility of being changed by another person. In this spirit of openness, we all hope to grow together and to let go of our anger, and our attempts to escape the walls that fortify us against one another.

Friday, July 14th

Silver was sentenced today for ten years. Homicide in the second degree. He pounded some guy to death in an abandoned house, while both of them were drunk out of their minds. Silver probably saved my life several years ago when his flying tackle took out a berserk, mentally ill, ex-boxer who was about to beat me up—bad.

He asked me to speak at his sentencing, giving a character reference. The irony of it all was not lost on anyone: a Catholic priest speaking for a convicted murderer, and asking the court for leniency. I was nervous as I made my pitch because the Judge was Mr. Frown Face, and the victim's family was sitting there in the front row, a mixture of disgust and revenge on their collective faces. I can't say I blamed them for being upset with me, for having that how-dare-you-look in their eyes. On the other hand, I know Silver. I have talked to him over lots of Nativity House cups of coffee and over those tables in sterile jail visiting rooms. I know his history of parental abuse, of the alcoholism, of relationships full—crammed full—of desperation, of the unforgettable moment when he leaped to defend my life. I also know that he would be the first to say that we must take responsibility for our acts.

Sometimes, we say there are people born with two strikes against them. In this man's case, he was a person born with nearly three strikes against him. And yet, in spite of all the personal chaos and obstacles, he has been like a boxer, who, having taken some devastating shots, stands up and keeps on moving. It has been that part which presses forward, that spark of self-actualization, that hunt for goodness within himself which he has entrusted to me. Trust is something he rarely allowed himself in his twenty-five years. But when he does trust, as he did with me, he reveals his secret: underneath all the tough-guy veneer, he is a gentle human being.

The family of the victim got what they wanted; the no-nonsense judge passed his sentence. Silver got a minimum of ten years. He was taken away by those faceless guards that do such things day after day after day. I sat there and wept with the two public defenders. They knew Silver's secret too.

Monday, August 14th

Priorities in our country vis-a-vis the poor can be so lop-sided. Yesterday, Texas Congressman Mickey Leland was killed in a helicopter crash. He was on yet another trip to Ethiopia in an effort to help resolve the hunger crisis in that poor country. There has been a huge media coverage. And rightly so, because this guy was a winner; his concern for the poor was the real thing. But, I wonder what would happen if a similar thing occurred in the USA? Would the newspaper headline say:

CONGRESSMAN DIES IN HELICOPTER CRASH
WHILE SEEKING TO RESOLVE POVERTY
PROBLEM IN TACOMA, WASHINGTON

Would the media lionize this hypothetical congressman who has died in the pursuit of a better life for the have-nots of our country? Would people translate our dead congressman's priorities into an American agenda?

I think not. I am cynical about priorities. Look what is happening almost right under the black and blue nose of Nativity House. Millions of dollars have been allocated to refurbish the old Tacoma Railroad Station in order to convert it to a federal court house. And all this transformation is taking place within sight of skid row where hundreds lack decent housing, employment training, educational opportunities, and adequate health care. What is going on here?

Something else, while I am complaining tonight. The same day that I read this article about the train station, one of our guests showed me a ticket he had received for urinating in public. Ironically, he was relieving himself in the same abandoned area where the court house facility will be constructed.

So there it is, there stands the reality of priorities: people frequently have no place to sleep—or urinate—and must stand in line at a drop-in center for baloney sandwiches, while down the street, the government builds a multi-million dollar facility, complete with a copper-plated dome. Mickey Leland, we need you here.

Saturday, September 9th

Eugene lives in a cheap apartment not too far from here. Like so many who are alone, he comes to Nativity House more for companionship than for food. As he sits there, stubby beard, gray hair, a book generally in his hand, I am always struck by his dignity. On the arthritically bad days, he carries a cane. This morning he waved me over to his chair, and, with acute embarassment, informed me that he had defecated in his pants. He asked me if I could I help him to the bathroom, and were there some extra pants? As we were quickly getting the game plan together, a quiet, young, unemployed laborer sitting next to Eugene, overheard our conversation and offered to help. So, one of Eugene's arms over his shoulder, he assisted Eugene to the bathroom, while I dug up some pants in the clothesroom. Once they arrived at the bathroom, this stranger-companion helped Eugene clean himself up.

I shall have that image locked in my brain forever: the old man, his pants full of shit, leaning on the unassuming young man, the two of them shuffling down the hallway. They were like two warriors coming out of battle, the stronger of the two bearing his wounded companion.

Monday, September 11th

Little John has been on the streets for a long time. He is a loner, a chronic alcoholic. He never opened up until he allowed Stacy to befriend him a few years ago, revealing a wonderfully simple man with a generous heart and a contagious sense of humor. He used to give her the unexpected gifts: little statues, food, earrings, and small change. He has a withering vocabulary that is sprinkled with some variation of "goddamned."

Not long ago, he announced to me that he had six hundred goddamned dollars in his goddamned pocket. What—said I, in astonishment—didn't he know the danger of packing that kind of money around on the streets? With a sly grin, he slowly extracted from a jacket pocket his false teeth: three hundred bucks for the uppers and three hundred bucks for the lowers.

Another time, he asked me to put some drops of medicine in his ears. We went into the office, and there, like some amateur bombardier, I made my run. Of course, John never stopped making editorial comments about the goddammed eardrops and my goddamed accuracy. As he left the office of the goddamned Doctor Smith, he was goddamned grateful.

I am always happy when I see him come through our doors.

Tuesday, September 26th

I am now moving into my sixth autumn at Nativity House. We have a good staff. Two new Jesuit Volunteers, Betty and Joe, have joined us to complement the experience of Carol and Pat. I am mentally tired. There are signs of wear and tear. Technically, I am at the top of my abilities, but I have noticed that it takes longer and longer to process the events of the day. There are moments when it is difficult to concentrate, when I am using enormous amounts of energy to be present to some of our guests.

When I ponder my relationships on the streets, I fear that I will become jaded. I don't think that has happened; my love and passion for our guests remains strong and true. I must monitor myself well this year and listen to the feedback of staff and friends.

Friday, September 29th

There are many humbling experiences when I share in another's honesty about him or herself. I listen to a brother or sister looking squarely at the unhappiness they have caused themselves and others and, in that process, I am left in awe. This happens frequently when a recovering alcoholic comes to me to work through Step Four and Step Five of the AA Twelve Step Program.

Luther phoned me, wanted to talk. We did not know each other. He knew of me through some of his AA acquaintances and wanted to do Steps Four and Five. We spoke quietly in the chapel where he worked off of a carefully-thought-through document in his nervous hands, the result of his "making a searching and fearless moral inventory" of himself and the desire "to admit to God, to himself and to another human being the exact nature of his wrongs."

As many times as I have been privileged to hear an alcoholic enter into the perilous, relentless, and liberating process of these Steps, I always come out the other side of the process in a state of admiration. It was not Luther's grocery list of destructive acts that floored me, nor the twisted nature of his past life. What touched me was his willingness to move forward, to refuse—any longer—to go it alone with his disease, and to reach into the depth of his inner feelings, thoughts, hopes, and resources.

Something wonderful and huge emerged in all his stutterings and tears, something very human and rich. I thought of the truth so well expressed by the poet Gerard Manley Hopkins: ". . . . for all this, nature is never spent;/ there lives the dearest freshness deep down things."

I came away from that session with Luther moved by his honesty and grateful to God for the spirit of courage and life that this man had claimed right before my dumbstruck heart. It was another sign of the Higher Power living and acting on the streets.

Sunday, October 1st

Leigh died yesterday of AIDS. I went to the hospital to visit him only to be told that he was dead. He was vulnerable to the disease, given the way he lived his life. I felt so alone walking away from the hospital. I wanted to scream as I left the lobby, or cry. Something. I remember him as a kind man. He was always perceptive enough to address the pain he saw in someone else, even when he knew his own life was fading fast. To say that I shall miss him simply does not express the loss.

I returned to the same hospital last night to see Myrna. A drug dealer had punished her by dragging her with his car, her arm caught in a rolled-up window as she was making a drug transaction. She was in intensive care: fractured pelvis, legs, shoulder, and half her scalp torn off. When I entered her room, she was conscious, in spite of all her injuries and the miles of tubes coming out of her broken body. We held hands. I wasn't sure what to say, but gently let her know that I was there and cared for her, and that I would pray with her. She squeezed my hand in response. Tears came down her face, and with my free hand I wiped them away with a tissue.

Her four teenage kids and her brother were in the waiting room. I spoke to them before I left. Anyway you look at it, the road to recovery is going to be a long one, and this family is going to suffer. It is terrifying to see what drugs can do.

Sunday, October 15th

Because there has been a sudden cold snap, reaching twenty-eight degrees this afternoon, Bernard is suffering. He is a well-known figure around town, tall, fierce-looking, often mumbling to himself. In all kinds of weather, he is barefoot and attired only in a sweatsuit. He has a child-like attitude with people he trusts, even though his general perceptions of things around him are full of delusional thinking. Periodically, he will come to me and rebuke me for not being the "Real Father Gary," and let me know that he resents my imitation of the real thing.

Today, Bernard asked me to be alone with him in the clothesroom where he sat me down and grabbed my hand and placed it on his cold feet, telling me there was something wrong with them. They were numb. He could not understand what was going on and wanted me to do something about it. At that point, I had to move through the mine field of Bernard's head. I knew he needed shoes, but I knew that he believed shoes to be evil and had a life of their own. He thought shoes would sew themselves into his stomach. I tried to explain to him that socks would keep his feet warm because they were not like shoes. In fact they would ward off the dreaded shoes. Bernard pondered my explanation which combined scientific knowledge and a profound knowledge of exorcism and agreed to wear the socks for the day, trusting more in me (the real Father Gary) than in my explanation. I gave him some snuggy wool socks that had "I hate shoes" written all over them.

Bernard turned to me as we were exiting the clothesroom and said, "Sometimes I want to turn into a bird and fly away." Don't we all, dear Bernard. Don't we all?

Thursday, November 16th

I awoke to National Public Radio this morning with the news that six Jesuits and two of their collaborators were murdered in El Salvador last night. All were connected with the University of Central America in San Salvador, all working in the turbulent world of social justice and the rights of the poor. They were the intellectual heart of the Salvadoran Church and leaders for change and reform in the tortured world of Central America. This news—this heartbreaking news—has simply frozen me all day.

At Mass later on, a Jesuit Novice, Terry, who has been working with us for a few months, broke down and wept uncontrollably. Rollin, a dark-eyed, black-bearded guest who comes every Thursday morning for this service, was seated next to Terry on the rug, and he reached over and took the Jesuit into his arms. They did not know each other, but Rollin, no stranger to suffering in his young life, spontaneously made his move toward Terry with the sensitivity and compassion born of an individual who knew pain. It did not end with Terry either, for later on he consoled some of the rest of us who were struggling with the grief of it all.

It was as if Rollin was breaking off a piece of himself and sharing that self with those in need. He was really the celebrant of the Eucharist this morning. He was the Christ walking the streets, comforting the comforters.

Monday, December 25th

At the Christmas Eve service last night, as we prayed for our needs, one of our guests, Becky, asked that we remember her "and all the other pregnant women of the streets." Her voice contained the hard and soft edges of uncertainty, discouragement, anger, fatigue, and anticipation. It was a prayer uttered from back in the crowd, yet it cast its power over the entire room, touching us all, touching this Christmas on the streets. And Becky's prayer connected us with the story of another expectant mother moving toward Bethlehem.

Nativity House takes its name from the Nativity of Christ. It tries to reflect the heart of Christ which is a heart for all: shepherds, kings, prostitutes, mentally ill, strangers, volunteers, staff, junkies, babies, terminally ill, cops, thugs, clergy, businessmen and women, handicapped, landlords, unbelievers, believers, and mothers-to-be seeking refuge.

Furthermore, as Christ's birth gives testimony to the forgiving and healing truth of God's love, likewise Nativity House takes its stand for all to see. It is this: "Come in, sort out, figure out; gather yourself, your wits, your strength; know that we believe that you are unique; know that we believe in your right to life and love."

The birth of Christ was, in a sense, God's best gift. I believe that what we do here—day in and day out—is give what is best in ourselves.

❖ *1990* ❖

Disguised Battery Acid

Friday, January 19th

The national TV program, *48 Hours*, was filming last week in Tacoma, doing a piece on drugs. One of our guests was very vociferous in her condemnation of what was going on, feeling that the media was using us.

I feel the same way. It is always a dilemma for me each time local television studios want to shoot some film on the homeless and ask to bring cameras into Nativity House. I would like our guests' story to be told, but I also know that television, by its very nature, will do a half-baked job. I always refuse the request. Street people, in a thirty-second film clip, can be judged, sentenced and executed, and their real story never told. If TV people want to tell the truth, then they need to spend many hours with their subjects, none of this slam-bam-thank-you-ma'am stuff.

I have had my stomach full of local TV celebrities who protest how badly they want to do the "real" story on the poor of the streets, yet never show up. They usually wind up on some insignificant street corner using it as a backdrop for some drug dealing or violence story.

TV spends millions—billions—on fantasy trips while the meaningful life stories, crying to be heard and seen, get buried away with their subjects in the obscure corners of America. In the world of megabuck TV advertising, no one is going to risk telling the truth.

Ray Bradbury's marvelous novel, *Fahrenheit 451,* tells of an oppressive society where underground individuals memorize an entire book because the dogmatic government is burning all books. Each person of the underground carries a story, a way to understanding, a gift for all. I think each of our guests is a unique story and deserves to be heard and cherished. There are no outlines here, no soundbites, no lives to be told in a fifteen-second summation.

Monday, February 12th

Nelson Mandela was released yesterday from his South African island prison, some twenty-seven years after he was imprisoned for speaking out against the institutional racism, apartheid, of his country. We watched it on TV. As blurry as our TV can be, as bad as the sound, as noisy as Sunday morning is, I have never seen such rapt attention on the part of our guests. There were so many levels of meaning, especially for our African-American guests. It was an event that left a bad taste. Although Mandela was free from incarceration, he was a long way from being free of the judgments placed on him because of his skin color.

Like the feelings of shame I have as a man, when a woman tells me of her sexual abuse at the hands of another man, so I go through a similar feeling when one of our guests of color tells me of their abuse at the hands of a white person: a job refused, a slur flung out of a passing car, an apartment that is not "available," the irrational hassle of a police officer, the unmistakable hostile look. I hate a racist attitude and the superficiality of it all. My greatest moments of wrath here are reserved for those fools who call a brother or a sister a "nigger," or a "chink," or a "wetback."

When my moments of shame and anger start to get me down, I talk to one of our guests who is not white; someone whom I trust and who trusts me. We discuss racism. I seek to understand how my head is screwed on in terms of the way I see the whole business, white man that I am. They are individuals who will tell it to me straight. They are human beings who have suffered because their skin is not white. These are hard discussions for me, but I have always felt that the dialogue is born and sustained in care and respect. Love does such things.

Lead us all, Nelson.

Thursday, March 1st

I was in Nativity House before dawn this morning, taking care of some paperwork (thank you notes to benefactors, figuring out some dates for Pest Control to spray for cockroaches, going over some business that I need to discuss with the Board). It was very still on Commerce Street. There had been a few hours of snow during the night, and the streets had taken on a clean white look, almost glowing in the street lamps.

I wound up praying in all the solitude. I was grateful for the chance to be with so many wonderful people. I prayed for all of my staff and people who help us out, up-front and behind the scenes. I asked that Nativity House be a place of healing and compassion, remembering the lines about Jesus who did not "break the crushed reed nor put out the smouldering wick." I sought help for all of us, so that our words would reflect God's truth, and our acts would reflect God's justice, and our love would reflect God's compassion.

Thursday, March 29th

Diane came to Nativity House often. She was a wonderful gift giver. Whatever the pain of her life, her drug addiction, her separation from her two daughters, it never obstructed her ability to give. When she encountered someone, there was no halfway deal. "I hate one-arm hugs," she would rebuke me and audaciously place my free arm around her. She gave us a furry, brown, stuffed dog, placing it on the ledge above the office, announcing, "It needed a home." When shy old Mac was around, it was Diane who brazenly and lovingly sat him down to a card game, an event riddled with her cackles and outrageous running commentary. The two of them were an apple and an orange, but they enjoyed each other. Old Mac loved it in all his simplicity.

A week ago, she died. Thirty-three. Dead. Questionable circumstances. On the street, the word is that she fixed on an eight-ball (cocaine and heroin), and it was too drug-pure for her system to handle. Another less reliable rumor is that she used some disguised battery acid.

I went to her funeral today, a graveside service at a little cemetery on the south side. It was a quiet service, the early spring breeze moving gently through the trees. Her sisters, brother, and mother were present, as well as her two daughters whom she had seen so infrequently. The rabbi, who had known Diane her entire life, spoke eloquently, "Her goodness was a benediction on all our lives."

We were good friends, Diane and I. We knew each other between the two cities of dark and light, hope and despair, the straight world and drug world. Three weeks ago, she said "I love you, Gary, but not in a sexual way; you and your staff are some of the few people I know who are not trying to fuck me." That same day she gave me two little framed pictures of her and Mac. One of the staff had photographed them in the middle of a card game. She instructed me to give them to her daughters "should anything happen."

I gave them to the family to be given to the daughters. They were wonderful photos of the Nativity House cardsharks: smiling Diane and befuddled, tickled Mac.

I knelt for a few moments at the graveside, then walked under the trees to my car. It is hard to imagine that I will never see her again.

Monday, April 2nd

Many families are on the streets at one time or the other. I am always proud of my staff for the love that they lavish on the children. Even though this is not a good place for kids, and even though they do not remain long, we establish some wonderful relationships with these little persons. Often the parents are so preoccupied with other things, like where they will sleep that night, that I think they lose the ability to be children with their children.

Ronnie is this wonderful, perpetual-movement, let's-jump-on-Father-Gary-or-Pat little boy of eight years. He comes by periodically with his equally affectionate ten-year-old sister and their parents. The mom and dad were on the streets in the mid-eighties until they got settled, but whenever they are downtown, they come by to see us. The children are very special.

Ronnie's mother called me several days ago in tears. The little guy, on his bike, had come barrelling out of an alley right into the path of a horrified and helpless motorist. By the time all the surgery was over, it was clear that he had suffered brain stem damage, lung contusions, and a broken right femur.

It was excruciating to go into that intensive care ward and look at his little body, so broken. He used to wrap himself around me and try to squeeze the breath out of me. I was there to be some support for the family, but I think that night I was as crushed and bewildered as anyone. When I left, I sat in my car in the hospital parking lot and I tried to get a hold of the enormity of what had happened to my little Ronnie. I sobbed into the steering wheel.

During the three days of coma, I sat next to Ronnie's bed, talking to him and holding his hand. He came out of it a few days ago, and today slowly looked at me with his unfocused eyes and whispered my name. My tears answered.

The prognosis is uncertain. He is young, and with good rehabilitation and lots of love, he will be able to make progress toward wholeness. It is going to be unspeakably tough on his parents.

Friday, April 13th

There has been an abundance of correspondence over these past several years with people in prison. I try to keep the letters going, especially to people in the state and federal prison systems. Being incarcerated for a long stretch can accentuate loneliness in an already very lonely environment. Lots of honesty and wisdom comes to me in these letter exchanges, and, too, we have been able to do a few favors out here for our prison friends.

Buddy wrote recently; he is a loveable guy—when he is sober. When he is intoxicated, he is obnoxious, and more than once the staff had to kick him out of Nativity House. He once spat in my face. And he has given me many gifts. He is now doing time in a state penitentiary for bank robbery and manslaughter. He has some amazing talents, including a facility for teaching English, cutting hair and signing for the deaf. His father was deaf. Yesterday, one of Buddy's letters arrived:

> You guys at Nativity House are definitely not of this present world. And I'm sure you'll be exposed and the greatest award of recognition will be given to you. And being the way your staff is, Gary, you will probably share the award. I'll bet anything the passing around will be called communion and you will change the bread and wine of your love into something living and wonderful and hand it out.
>
> PS: I take responsibility for being an asshole and spitting on you.
>
> PPSS: I'm sorry.
>
> PPPSSS: I love you.

Sunday, April 15th

This has got to fall under the category of Believe-It-Or-Not. Sunday afternoon. Packed house. Lots of hungry people waiting for lunch. Michael, a lean and gaunt forty-seven-year-old, holding his rib cage, asked to see me alone. His face was full of pain. We went into the chapel. The day before he had tried to pull off a robbery in a small town south of Tacoma and had failed. Not only did he bungle the robbery, but he took a hit from some shotgun pellets as he was making his get-away. Underneath his brown leather jacket, he wore a blood-soaked T-shirt, and in his waistband was tucked a thirty-eight revolver. He warned me not to call the police or paramedics because he had no intention of being taken back to prison again. He said he had spent 22 years in prison, and even now, he had some outstanding warrants for his arrest.

In all his obvious pain, he said he wanted to talk with me, specifically because he knew that I was a priest, and, through the street grapevine, he had heard that I was someone who could be trusted. So, with the noise of hundreds of people outside the chapel leaking into our conversation, and in the midst of his wheezing, with that big revolver in his bloody belt staring me in the face, he proceeded to unload his terrible secret. It was a death-bed confession. I had never heard anything like it before.

We finished. I tried to dissuade him from leaving and to think twice about his refusal for medical assistance, but to no avail. With a final grimace, he grabbed my hand, pulled himself up, gave me an embrace and slowly moved out the door. I had, of course, a responsibility to guard what he had shared with me, but I never promised not to make an effort to save his life, so I called a policeman friend of mine. By the time he arrived, Michael had vanished off the streets.

The next day, he called me from a hospital. The need to deal with the pain had been greater than his fear of returning to prison, and so he had checked into Emergency. He sounded more coherent and had a kind of I'll-take-my-chances-attitude. He thanked me and said that he had made other deeper decisions about his life.

Monday, May 14th (A cottage on the Puget Sound)

The entire staff, Betty, Joe, Pat, Carol, and I, has been spending a few days away. It is an opportunity to give ourselves time to talk about our efforts at Nativity House. It's a mental health break in which we can pray and eat and relax together. I enjoy these moments with them; they bring their own unique hearts and fresh viewpoints to the task of building our mission on the streets.

I always have this lingering fear that Nativity House will stand still and not grow and continue to reach out, that it will become comfortable with the reality of the homeless because I have become comfortable. For me, there is the temptation not to reach out to the unreachable person, not to challenge someone who is not claiming his or her potential, and not to call the City of Tacoma to its responsibilties toward the poor of the streets. There is always the possibility of passing over the beauty of a

given individual because I am too preoccupied or too distracted.
I even fear that I will lose track of God.

Having expressed all these fears around where I may stumble, it is to the credit of my staff that they have not occurred.

Sunday, May 20th

I sometimes watch people who work here wrestle with the angel. The stuff of relationship on the streets is not easy, but it is wonderful to see them take it on. I asked Carol to write something about the struggle. She wrote in a recent newsletter:

A key to understanding the heart of Nativity House is that we try to create an atmosphere where healing can begin. And, more important than this, people need to know that they deserve to be healed. We try to affirm people by telling them that they are special and by treating them accordingly. They need to know that they can move beyond quick fixes. Gradually healing occurs, and our guests are empowered to move through the pain by dying to it and rising beyond to a renewed self of value and hope.

It is a beautiful gift when we are blessed to witness such a transformation. At the height of her pain, Bethany was covered with sores from drug use; she was prostituting; she was underweight, recently raped and had just been hit by her boyfriend for looking so poorly. One day, I held her silently as she was bleeding from her mouth and moaning in pain. Within weeks, she was in a recovery house, staying clean and mending ties with her family. She stopped in daily to proudly state how many days she had been clean and to hug each one of us on the staff and to tell us that she loved us. And then she went on her way. She is in a treatment facility now with over sixty days of being drug-free. She looks healthy and radiant.

Bethany brings meaning and life to the story of Christ's pain, suffering, and resurrection. Very few changes are this dramatic, but all steps toward healing and choice for life are precious and need to be celebrated.

Tuesday, June 5th

The Great Nativity House Plumbing Crisis of 1990 began when we noticed an odor around the kitchen and the bathroom. It was apparently coming from below where there is nothing but an empty floor in our rented three-story building. Given other things on my mind, I wrote it off to warm-weather street smells, or a dead rat. Besides, it diminished as the day progressed. Finally, I sent Pat and Joe down through the trap door which connects the first and second floor, in order to check out the mysterious and rapidly-becoming-more-powerful odor.

The two explorers ascended from down below and Pat said, "Well, Buddy, the good news is that we are not dealing with dead rats; the bad news is that the basement is full of shit." What had happened was that the sewage drainage pipe had plugged up at the street level, backing everything up to the toilets on the floor below. All of our sewage was downstairs. It had apparently accumulated for weeks. During the remainder of the day, a tanker truck suctioned and removed over 500 gallons of raw human waste.

The problems were just beginning, not to mention the expense. Before it was all over, we had gone through the tanker truck people (they should have rented NASA space suits just to cope with the smell), the Rotor Rooter trouble shooters, a city street construction crew, an independent contractor, and a lot of talk between myself and our Board Chairperson, Dave. Fortunately, Dave knew his way around the world of construction and city officialdom.

It went on for seven days. They tore up walls, floors, sidewalks, and streets—indeed, they were ten feet down into the main street of Tacoma.

Of course, we stopped using all water and shut down that innocent but indirect culprit, our toilet. Between the styrofoam cups, plastic utensils, and paper plates, we probably set the ecology movement back two years.

One of our guests, never a person to miss the humor of anything, came in one day during the crisis and gave me one of the baseball caps that has printed across its front: SHIT HAPPENS.

The crisis led to lots of scrambling to find a place "to go." One woman told me that she had used the downtown Sheraton a couple of times, but preferred our little, bootlegged, unisex toilet. "It was more comfortable," she said.

When all the streets were filled back in and all the pipes were clear and we could take the OUT OF ORDER sign off the restroom door, I felt like throwing a party. Shit may happen but, please, not this way anymore.

Saturday, July 7th

Old Earl died at the VA hospital yesterday. He was one the first persons I met here, a craggy-faced veteran of life with a gift for gab. He used to own and run a service station in nearby Auburn until alcohol and development caught up with him, and the business folded. He collected aluminum cans to supplement his social security, and it was a common sight to see him trudging down the street, plastic bag of cans slung over his hunched-up shoulders. He slept always, whatever the weather, in his old, beat-up Chevy Pickup, a relic from his service station days He could go on for hours about the good old times, but as the crowd became more young and more diverse, he found fewer and fewer listeners. Slowly, his mental faculties eroded, and he started dragging one foot; it was the result, I'm sure, of a flurry of baby strokes. I last saw him here as he stormed out the door, as fast as his unwilling foot would allow, angry that I had asked him to change his clothes which were beginning to smell. I am told that he did not last long at the VA once he arrived, a fact which did not surprise me, since he loved his independence.

The same day that we learned the news of Earl, young Jennie came in, newborn baby nestled in her proud arms. It was one of those moments when I see the alienation and controlled despair of the streets give way to the energy and power and magic of a child. Jennie's daughter was passed around to various guests; it was one of the tender rituals of a new parent.

The death of Earl. The birth of a baby. We are privileged to be part of the whole cycle of life, in all of its joy and sorrow. Nativity House creates a space where the poor can mourn and where they can celebrate.

Sunday, July 22nd

Last night, we had our annual dinner for the many groups and individuals who give their time and treasure to Nativity House. The Board of Directors always throws this night of feeding and recognition. As usual, they did a superb job. It is an occasion, too, for me to thank personally all the people and to give recognition to our departing staff. In this case, all of my staff was leaving.

I shall miss this staff. I'll miss their pursuit of the truth, their ability to laugh, their love, and sense of justice. Such qualities never fail to be an inspiration to me. I will miss their willingness to deal with my moods. They have been able to act in a way which encouraged me to make the decisions that a director needs to make, but were never bamboozled by the myth of the street priest who can make no mistakes. So it has been that they have owned Nativity House, too, and were never afraid to offer opinions and challenge me. Indeed, they saw that it was incumbent upon them to do so.

Another wonderful thing about most of my staffers, a quality which every director in the world would envy, is that they had mastered the art of laughing at my jokes, even when the jokes were not funny.

We can't go it alone on the streets. We simply have to depend on each other, love each other, believe in the growth and talents of the team. It is in the living out of this truth that I have come to have a great affection for my staff. Thomas Merton wrote the line I often quote to myself when I think of them: "The good that you do will come not from you, but from the fact that you have allowed yourself, in the obedience of faith, to be used by God's love."

Saturday, August 18th

Cops II. Dropping by almost daily, Officers Mike and Jim have become welcome guests at Nativity House. Mike is a tall, big-boned guy, always ready with a funny quip, yet someone who is attentive and present to the most obscure person. Jim, a prematurely gray and handsome man, is reserved, yet friendly. I always sense that he is aware of everything that is going on around him, even though he may be focused in on a conversation.

The streets need a special kind of heads-up, feet-on-the-ground type of cop. He or she has to be firm and flexible, capable of dealing gently with the most bewildered and frightened individual while prepared to use force with the dangerous and violent. The best response I have seen to the police down here is when they are honest, fair, and human. Mike and Jim know that many street people like them because they exhibit these qualities.

I have come to respect them, and I am the guy who over the years has had an abundance of confrontations with Tacoma's "Finest." I appreciate their goodness with the guests from the streets; I admire their courage in facing the daily possibility that they could be killed in the the line of duty—and the streets can be a fearful line of duty. I also am grateful that they have worked hard at understanding Nativity House, and why it is a harbor for so many, including, obviously, many with criminal records.

The unstated but obvious rap on these two is this: they believe in the dignity and value of each person they encounter.

Monday, August 20th

I am beginning my seventh year. A good staff has come to replace the old: Pam and Kevin, who are members of the Jesuit Volunteer Corps, and Kay, a long-time volunteer who has decided to join us as a full time staffer. It looks like a promising crew.

I wonder if this will be my last year? I have the usual excitment, but underneath there is this worn-out feeling. There is a sense, too, that I may need to stand back, to stretch myself. Sometimes it comes as something as general as a desire to go blow my mind in another culture, so that I can return and look at the streets in a fresh way.

I am struggling with another issue, too. The Jesuits more and more are talking about a lived-out commitment to the poor. It is one thing to fight against all forms of human poverty; it is another and more demanding reality to go beyond that and live with the poor, to share in their lives and their sufferings. I am not doing that yet. I live on the safe side of the Catholic Left. In part, I am facing the issue, here, on the streets, but stepping back may be the only way I can confront something deep inside of me that keeps inviting and probing.

Thursday, August 31st

The coroner's call came on a busy Nativity House afternoon. Did I know Tracy? Did I know where her relatives could be reached? We had learned of her murder a few days ago. Her bloated body was pulled out of the Puget Sound. We all felt grief and helplessness over the violent death of one we knew. This death was one of the toughest to take. I don't think I am going to be able to take many more.

Tracy and I used to talk about her life, her pain, her future. She had a sharp mind and a tongue to match. Underneath her grave and searching look, I always saw a beautiful woman, longing to be reached. Sometimes, through all the surface hardness and trembling defensiveness, the tears would break through.

In the end, her family was found, and her remains were sent to them. But here on the streets, we needed some kind of closure to the loss. The memorial service we held one Friday afternoon was preceded by two baskets of yellow flowers sent by some friends—old friends from the past of better days. Inside Nativity House, as we began with Psalm 23, there was a circle of faces and hearts of those who knew her. Close or distant, all came to say hello and goodbye. Around were many of the addicts who knew Tracy's battle with heroin; present were some caring friends who went to school with her many years ago; near the wall stood the two policemen, Jim and Mike, alone with their thoughts about a human being, not a criminal; sitting in front of me was an ex-husband; near the kitchen sat a well-dressed woman who four years ago had lost her daughter to the violence of the streets. In the back of the room stood a burned-out Nam Vet who announced the pain of his grief and an anger that spoke of vengeance; off to my left, hunched over, sat a mentally ill woman, mumbling about a lost daughter.

Some remembered Tracy's sense of humor. Indeed, Tracy used to poke fun at my pensive face: "Why so serious, Father?" One friend, once involved in prostitution, remembered her "care and love." Near the end of our memorial, one individual leaped up and asked if he could lead us in the Lord's Prayer. And so we all stood, grasped hands, and remembered a friend, placing the chaos and mystery of this death in God's hands.

It was important to have this memorial for Tracy. The Church on the streets must speak to her life and death. It must create those moments where we can mourn together and have our grief held in the arms of the community. The Church, too, has to remind the world that Tracy is not to be reduced to the "drug addict and active prostitute" categorization which an indifferent newpaper tagged on her. The Church must rather say, as our guests did so eloquently that Friday afternoon, that here is a human being, here is a loved child of the Creator.

Friday, September 14th

The truth that it may be time to leave street ministry—for a break—has been pursuing me more and more these days. I am gently taking a look at myself. My biggest fear in serving the poor of the streets has been that I might develop a form of hanging-on, plodding-along style, one that will lose track of the individual in the midst of the endless, ever-changing street population. That has not occurred. But what is clear is that I am tired—deep down—and I am running out of steam.

This is a hard fact to look at, given the pride I have in myself around being a self-starter, endlessly capable of re-charging my battery—in a word, indestructible. But who am I kidding? Certainly not my friends who see the signs: fatigue, the furrowed brow, a short fuse, a tendency to lose my concentration. Did Tracy spot it?

I am not running away when I ponder these things; it is more discernible as a going toward. What is the Holy Spirit calling me to? It is a love affair which I do not understand, but one to which I want to give myself.

I have been reading the life of John Henry Newman. There came a moment in his life, successful as he was, when it was time to make a switch. He knew of course that he was tired, but there was something else going on: a sense that his call was beckoning to something else. He wrote these words:

Keep Thou my feet; I do not ask to to see
The distant scene—one step enough for me.
Lead, kindly Light, Lead Thou me on.

Sunday, September 16th

Alfredo returned today. Last year, he was picked up by the Immigration Service and shipped back to Northern Mexico. Although he has worked in this country for nearly thirty-five years, his acquisition of legal documents has always been hampered by the fact that he cannot prove his birth. A fire destroyed all such documents in his Mexican home village. Like so many who have been deported, he crossed over again and made the long and harrowing trip back to the Northwest. He is a wonderful man, always willing to talk—in Spanish—even though he describes himself as *ando solo*, someone who walks alone. Pat used to say that Alfredo was teaching him Spanish, so that Pat could better understand Alfredo's story which is one full of hardship and loneliness.

This year, we have seen a steady increase of Mexicans and Central Americans who have entered the country illegally, fleeing from the political and economic hard times of their homelands. In America, for the most part they take menial jobs, often sending a portion of what little money they do make back to their impoverished families. Many, like Alfredo, will make a point to contribute an offering to Nativity House. Because they do not speak English, they often fall prey to greedy employers who will try to make a buck off their backs. And given the prejudice which exists toward people of color, plus the language deficiency, the road is not an easy one. In spite of all this, they are, for the most part, a gentle and grateful group. They are appreciative when we speak to them and pray for them in their own tongue. So little can mean so much when you are in another culture.

Alfredo ribbed me that I was looking very old, in fact he thought I might have passed him in years. I countered that his vision was clearly fading, now that he had passed ninety. We are all happy to see him again, *salvo y sano*, safe and sound.

Sunday, September 23rd

Every Sunday afternoon for the past several weeks, a local, heavy-duty evangelical group has been setting up across the street and launching into a couple of hours of spirited gospel singing and Bible-waving preaching. I often sit down with the rest of the troops on the sidewalk and listen as they shout directly at Nativity House, that Babylon fleshpot of downtown Tacoma. They haven't a clue who I am, sitting there, listening, my

Oakland A's baseball cap on, probably yet another sign of our need for salvation.

The street folks, for the most part, see these groups as well-meaning, but disconnected from the real world they seek to convert. Our guests have an expression which describes this hard-sell approach to Christianity: it is called "ear-banging." It comes from the practice of some skid row missions which require people to listen to a sermon before they are given food. You don't listen, you don't eat.

What good does it do to talk about being born again to a man or woman trying to survive, trying to obtain minimal food and clothing? What good is a quick fix on religion to a person preoccupied with obtaining a job? How can a mother or father be expected to take seriously beautiful and eternal truths when their family has no place to sleep this night? For me, the ear-banging approach to evangelization is, at best, disconnected from life, and, at worst, it perpetuates a phony Christianity which is humming sweet Jesus while cities are savaged by despair and poverty.

As I sat there last Sunday, mulling these things over in my head, distracted periodically by cynical remarks of street folks, one of the church members began to pamphlet all of us, awkwardly assuring us that his church was making a long range commitment to "you people." I wearily accepted yet another pamphlet knowing that, like so many others, these folks will leave once the cold weather comes. So much for commitment. I understand why institutional religion is looked on with such cynicism by the people of the streets.

The Church's credibility is directly connected with its permanent solidarity with the poor.

Saturday, September 29th

Richard is a leprechaun of a man, with a nose that has been broken an uncountable number of times. He has scarred eyebrows which are the result of many intoxicated falls. Quite frankly, I've ignored him whenever he has made an appearance.

He is usually under the influence of alcohol, rendering conversation impossible. But today, we talked. He was sober, sipping coffee, sitting quietly on one of the couches.

It was an astounding conversation. He is a pensioner, holds a graduate degree from the University of New Mexico and used to work as a civil engineer. In his professional life, he has done jobs from Alaska to Iran. At one point in our discussion, he suggested that we walk outside, and there, strolling past empty buildings and aging warehouses, he recounted, choking with emotion, the history of growing up in Northern California. He told me of his abusive, alcoholic father who once tipped an dinner table full of food on him, because Richard started to weep. His father rebuked him, "No son of mine will be a crybaby!" So ended, at the age of eight, the expression of Richard's feelings and ignited those underground engines of repression that can power alcoholism and a lifetime of anger and depression.

The honesty of Richard's Commerce Street tears opened some of the doors of my own struggles rooted in the unresolved issues of personal history. Often, as children, we accept the fraud that our meaning—who we are—is derived from the negative behavior inflicted on us. So if the big person—a parent or authority figure—communicates that we are not good, then we can judge ourselves to be intrinsically evil. We can spend a lifetime acting out of a feeling of self-deprecation, self-hatred, self-disbelief.

Hopefully, our meaning comes from ourselves, but that is so difficult to live out when one grows up in a reign of terror.

Sometimes I look around at our guests, and I see many who have been the recipients of the incomprehensible anger and negative judgments of parents. That may not explain all their lives, but it certainly helps me to see the wounds they carry. And my own. The wound of having a table crash down on top of you—pushed by a crazed father—heals slowly, tortuously.

Friday, October 19th

Many of our guests, Cincinnati Reds fans, are mercilessly ragging me about the Oakland A's, my team, as they—the A's—

are getting chewed up in the World Series. People are serious baseball fans here. One guy came to me, and, with all the poise of a Las Vegas gambler, plunked a quarter on the table and made a bet for his Reds, giving me ridiculous odds. It is amazing and wonderful how people get to know my weaknesses and have fun with my blind, irrational loyalty to Oakland. But the die is cast. It looks like Cincy in a sweep. Imagine, Oakland being swept.

Suddenly I have a special empathy for Chicago Cub fans. One Cubs devotee came stealthily into the kitchen where I was cooking and offered his sincere condolences. He said, "I know how you feel, Father."

Wednesday, October 24th

Some glances on this day.

The police brought in a well-dressed young woman who was found disoriented and wandering around downtown. She was stoned on some drug. She was also very paranoid. Did the staff know her? No, we did not. Could she rest here until she came down? Yes, of course. We call the suburbanites who come downtown looking for dope on Friday and Saturday, "Weekend Warriors." They are out of their league, frequently ripped off, paying incredibly large amounts of money, and they are risking their lives either from bad dope or bad guys. This woman was lucky. Eventually, she settled down and left, refusing to give any name.

I broke up an altercation between Ken and Lamont. On the surface, its cause was a spilled cup of coffee on an extended foot. Deeper level cause: take all the boredom, the lack of privacy, the stinking clothes, the endless noise and a feeling that no one cares, and one is pushed to a flashpoint by the most minimal act. People sometimes don't know why they are fighting; the urge to swing is stronger than the ability to size up the situation.

This afternoon, a formation of four helicopters swooped over downtown; their engines were deafening. I looked over at two Nam Vets huddled in the corner, not far from where I was talking on the phone. They stopped chatting and stared out the window. Their eyes had that look of another time and another place.

Thursday, November 15th

Al, a tall, well-spoken man, pushing fifty, carries on a digni-fied conversation. Occasionally, when he was here, he read scripture for the Sunday morning church service. A couple of months ago, his problem with drugs caught up with him, and he wound up in a Seattle jail. He was sent to a strict drug rehab clinic, which required total adherence to the program or he would be returned to the slammer. A few nights ago, he left AWOL and bobbed and weaved his way back to Nativity House. He needed to get back to Atlanta where his people were and where he had no criminal record. He asked if I could I help him.

I was in the dilemma again. Do I respect the letter of the law, or do I try to read the heart of the individual? Am I dealing with the delusion of the addict or the honesty of someone who just needs a break? In this case, I tried to outline the options which Al was facing, including the fact that he might be on the run for a long time.

I helped him with busfare to Denver; we couldn't afford it, but my hunch was that it was the right thing to do.

Saturday, November 24th

Bruce approached me as I was standing by the coffee pot. He had a round baby face, very short hair, and was wearing this outsized trenchcoat; I'd guess he was in his mid-twenties. He said, "Ban me."

"Why?" I asked.

He responded, "Because I deserve to be. In fact, I deserve to be punished, killed, and buried."

I took him aside, suggesting that before I ban him, it might be a good idea for us to talk. We went to the office and then, as we reached the door, he began to smash his head into the wall. He was pounding his head like a battering ram, trying to get through all the plaster and wood and metal to the other side. I yelled to Pam to call the Crisis Team from the Health Department, while Kevin and I tried to restrain this poor guy from seriously hurting himself. He settled down and cried a lot and eventually was taken to the hospital for observation. I had never seen him before.

Most reliable studies suggest that almost one-third of the homeless of America are chronically mentally ill or have had one or more mental hospital episodes. It is painful to see so many chronic or borderline mentally ill on the streets. They are so vulnerable, so pathetically lost and so alone. And their illness often leads away from friends and family relationships.

What can Nativity House do as it finds itself a harbor for so many of these unfortunate brothers and sisters? We are very protective. We insure that basic needs are taken care of, and that they are not abused by some of the human predators who lurk on the streets. We talk with them; even in the most crazed talk, one finds the recognizable pieces of a crushed heart. We love them, believing that our constant care will be an island of meaning in their world, where even the most simple of events and relationships can be dangerous and bewildering. We believe that they are children of God, no less than any of us who may have had better breaks along the way.

There are clearly moments when a person is a danger to himself and others. Our task at that point must be to alert the appropriate health professionals who can respond and determine the best way to remove the danger.

It is difficult at times, but we must continue to reach out to the mentally ill and speak out for them. This is especially true in America. Our culture does not like to face illness and is uncomfortable with most forms of disability. If Nativity House is to exist at all, then it must exist for the most marginal of our marginalized brothers and sisters.

Monday, December 17th

This last week, I have decided to leave Nativity House. I will leave next summer. It is indisputable that I am weary. There have been some signs that my body has had it, telling me in effect that enough is enough. To back this up, there were some strange readings on a routine electrocardiogram test I underwent recently during my annual check-up. Another sign?

It is going to be painful to act on this decision. I love the people I meet and come to know each day.

I trust God is leading me. More and more, I realize how much God has invaded my life, seized it, directed it. My life as a priest, street worker, my love for my dearest friends, my thoughts, my most intimate decisions about life are all connected directly and indirectly with God's movement within me.

Now, within this new turn, within this decision to leave Nativity House, as hard as it will be, I want to be open, trusting. Kierkegaard:

> You love us first, O God and
> When we wake in the morning
> And turn our soul toward you—
> You are there first, waiting.

Tuesday, December 25th

What a memorable Christmas Eve Mass we had last night. It was a packed house of our street guests and visitors from various organizations and churches. It was a thrill to hear everyone sing, "O Come All Ye Faithful." Afterwards everyone hung around for coffee and cookies, chatting away. We left without cleaning up, giving the once-a-year-cookie-crumb feast to the ever opportunistic roaches. They were probably crazed and dribbling from whatever they call their mouths when the lights went out and they found that haul.

Today, Pam wore an outrageous Rudolph the Reindeer red nose as she distributed our gifts of stuffed socks, compliments of a wonderful benefactor. His care for the poor matches, and goes beyond, his personal wealth. While Kevin, Kay, Neil and I were organizing dinner, the Christmas tree was blinking on and off, the chattering and joking at a high pitch. This Christmas was exceptional.

❖ *1991* ❖

A Giraffe Done in Crayola

Wednesday, January 30th

I met Posey around 1987. He had followed in some young hot shot who had stolen his son's sneakers. I spoke to him as he sat calmly in a corner, having learned the whole story from the fear-filled thief.

Posey had a gun. He told me, respectfully, that nothing was going to happen inside of Nativity House, but the man was going to return those shoes, or he wasn't going to return anything for the rest of his short life. I brought the two of them together and made it clear that I thought Posey was not kidding. The shoes were returned. Posey thanked me and promised never to enter Nativity House again with his revolver.

He died three nights ago. AIDS. When I saw him last at the hospital, he was in an isolation room, alone, and in a coma. It was the home stretch. I held his hand and spoke to him over the wheezing of his breathing. We had come to know each other, Posey and I, over these years, and I was grateful for his friendship as I knew he was for mine.

I said to him something like this: "Posey, we both know you are dying, and I want to tell you before you go that I am grateful for you, for your cheerful laugh, and for your ready support of Nativity House. I appreciated the moments when you helped to chill out some problems. People listened to you. I know your heart is good, and I know God loves a good heart. I promise to remember you and pray for you."

I was sitting holding Posey's hand when his daughter came in.

He died during the night.

Posey was a Vietnam Vet, and he told me that he was into a lot of shady stuff in Tacoma after his return. Shortly before we first met, his wife had been murdered and dumped onto his front lawn. It was a case of drug people playing hardball. Pay back time from his past.

As he became more ill, he became more of a person of faith. He told me once, "I know it sounds kind of chickenshit, Father, getting religious when things are falling part, but *you* know I am

not chickenshit. I just want to face my God honestly and admit
the stupid stuff in my life."

Friday, February 22nd

During the Christmas holidays, Jolie had invited me over
for dinner. She was now a long time into recovery. With us at
the meal was her fiance, a gentle and hardworking man, several
years into recovery himself, someone who loved her very much.
While we were eating, they popped the question: would I officiate at their wedding? I gulped and said yes. Oh, yes.

Tonight, I married them. There stood Jolie, who once described her life as a blackness, where there was no past, no future, not even a now; who, in that momentous Nativity House
clothesroom meeting long ago, was overwhelmed by drugs and
prostitution and self-disgust. There she stood, tall, radiant, pos-
sessing a clear-eyed beauty. She committed herself in love and
did so in freedom. In her promises of giving and receiving life,
she was, ultimately, renewing a pledge to herself.

If someone were to ask me what was the happiest moment
of my life on the streets, I will forever return to this moment. To
see someone I love not only crawl out of her darkness, but to
stand still, like I did alone in that room in Toronto years ago, and
turn toward the window—toward the morning's sunlight—has to
be one of the great consolations of my life. It makes all the dis-
consolate moments, all the failures, all the sickness, all the impossible and mad convolutions of human behavior, all the suffering—all of it—worth enduring again.

As I left the wedding party, Jolie and I stood outside for a
moment, holding each other. We really didn't say anything. We
both just sensed the truth of it all and the love and hope we had
for each other. She stood back, looked at me, and said, "You are
a big part of what has happened to me, Gary. Thanks." With
that she turned and returned to the party—through the door
where the light was pouring out.

Tuesday, March 12th

I spent an overnighter at the hospital going through some heart procedures, the result of that funny looking electrocardiogram I took last December. The results were negative. It turns out my heart signal is transmitted differently from the majority of people.

It was nice to be the recipient of so much care during those twenty-four hours: phone calls, a bottle of wine, a ton of cards, flowers, a teddy bear, and some good hugs. When I was rolled into my room following the angiogram procedure, there was a plate of Pam-made chocolate chip cookies sitting on my bed with a sign attached saying, "Delicious cookies for Gary." Several of my friends from the street, led by Alonzo, came up to check me out and gab. They laughed at the spectacle of the boss in those funny hospital jam jams, and those rascals devoured my delicious cookies.

During the night, in a quiet and relatively empty wing of the hospital, I didn't sleep much. Couldn't. I was staring directly into the paradox that can attend hospital nights: feeling elated over the gift of life and feeling frightened over the fragility of life. It was one of those hushed and stand-still moments when truth seeps in, gently, unobtrusively. I feel this way when I walk on the Pacific Beach or gaze from a vista point on Mount Rainier or when I hold an old friend in my arms.

The decision to leave Nativity House became more clear and firm in that Tacoma night. Physically and emotionally, I had hit the wall. It was time to stop. Yet, I wasn't worried about the next six months, either in terms of fatigue or in terms of the pain of separation. Any prospective darkness would be beaten back by the great consolation of my life: being loved in my fragility. There is the love of the poor of the streets who constantly evangelize me. There is the love of my closest friends who faithfully believe in me and support me. There is the love of God whose mercy steadily accompanies me in the contradictions of my life and whose spirit impels me to move foward to the next part of the journey.

Wednesday, March 20th

I notice that I am becoming irritable and touchy on occasion. I hung up on someone who called from jail, who accused me of snitching on him and causing his arrest. He yelled. I hung up. Later, I blew my stack at a fellow who was demanding some special treatment, unwilling to wait like the rest of us for a cup of coffee. He did a reciprocal stack-blowing at me, so I kicked him out, wondering who was the bigger jerk. Then I jumped all over yet another guy who was ogling and bothering some of our women guests. I told him if he wanted to act like an animal he could do so outside, and if he did not stop his behavior, he would not be allowed into Nativity House.

In all three cases, it was not that my response was off the mark; it was the manner in which I responded: an in-your-face, intimidating anger, using my verbal abilities and my position to hit harder than was necessary.

The feedback from the staff was helpful, inviting me to take a look at myself, reminding me of what I have taught them: stay with the issue and don't go after the person in a way that is fueled by my own hangups. If I were counseling myself I would say, "You are tired."

One guest, sensing a more relaxed attitude on my part, couldn't resist a cheerful shot across the bow this morning.

"Well, how's the human flamethrower today?"

I smiled and replied, "Cooling down, cooling down. With a little help from my friends."

Thursday, April 4th

Hans has faithfully come into Nativity House twice a month bearing donations. Today, again, a half-dozen donuts, some of his wife's homemade jam, five bucks, and a bundle of old *Reader's Digests*. Shortly after World War II, he came to this country from Europe, where he and his wife endured much suffering. He gives to the down-and-out because he has never forgotten that he was in a similar position once in his life.

Anyone who directs a center for the homeless will testify to many individuals who give constantly to that center with their time and talents, with their goods and money. Hans is but one example of this behind-the-scenes army.

Two retired men bring in a case of soup each month; an officer from the local army base and his wife show up every winter with dozens of pairs of warm gloves; three women are on the scene twice a month to wash dishes; a Weyerhauser executive, a voracious reader, keeps our bookshelves full of paperbacks; one gentleman walks in every Christmas Day and hands me a check for $2,000; a retired Air Force officer donates hours of computer time to keep our mailing list accurately updated. There are hundreds of people who make regular donations of money, and many nameless givers who walk in with bags of food. One day we received a year's supply of paper cups; another time, enough peanut butter for a couple of years.

The story goes on and on. As there are many groups who share with us, so there are these individuals, giving generously and quietly. It is enough that some brother or sister has been helped. The Body of Christ so often lives through kind and anonymous hands in the unsung corners of the world.

Friday, April 12th

"Rev, you got to *git down* so we can *git up*." So spoke Jefferson as I was preparing for Mass last Sunday. This man is a great towering angel who has come among us, spreading goodness and influence like the wind. Few of our guests over these seven years have been as affirming for me and for my staff.

Jefferson is a veteran of many things: military, marriage, business. He has succeeded, and he has failed. He has known the joy of having it together and the misery of using drugs. He possesses a deep rolling laughter, a voice that reaches all corners, and a hug that goes to the soul. The man is like a father to everyone.

Why is he here? It is hard to figure except that he loves Nativity House and knows the way of the streets even though he is living in a cheap apartment a mile from here. And he likes to be—as he says—"with my people," and with that expression he sweeps his hand around the room.

While I was thinking about Jefferson tonight, I thought of Ursula, a 22-two-year-old terminal cancer patient whom I had annointed in a Toronto hospital. I was a young priest and very nervous. I remember her, hours before she was to die, assuring me and comforting me and encouraging me in what I was doing. She was ministering to the minister.

Once in a while, someone comes to Nativity House who seems to have a mission to look after the staff. That person does nothing but laugh and do good. And that is everything. Jefferson is such a man.

Monday, April 15th

The women of the streets. If we can say that we discover ourselves in the presence of other persons, then I can say that I discover myself in the presence of the women of Nativity House. It seems this past week I have been affirmed, in many different ways, by the extraordinary group of women who have come our way.

Sandy, crying her eyes out over her drinking and broken relationships, brings me a rose at the end of the day; Leora, the bag lady, slips me a card that talks of how the staff saw something in her that was loveable—"somehow"; Peggy, wounded and kicked around, expresses her concern for my tired face; Louise, developmentally disabled, never misses a hello or goodbye; Violet brings her gifts of cookies and flowers; Joyce speaks gratefully for the time I spent with her; Lisa sneaks me into the chapel so I can put my hand on her 6-month-pregnant stomach; Alisha gives me great hugs and thanks me for the Mass on Sunday; Georgia calls from jail and has her entire wing yell, in unison, "Hi, Father Gary!"

In a street world dominated by men, machismo, and hard edges, it is in the presence of our remarkable women guests where I have discovered best what is gentle and sensitive in my heart.

Wednesday, April 17th

Elijah was at the door this morning when I opened up, face drawn, shirt and pants covered with blood, a cut on his arm that was huge and deep. It looked like it had gone through the muscle. He had been walking all night with this wound. Apparently, there had been an altercation with his girlfriend, and she had pulled a butcher knife. And used it.

He had come to talk. For the entire night, he had been driven by fury and revenge, but on the other hand, he did not want to kill anyone. What did I think?

So we talked, Elijah, the son of a Mississippi sharecropper, and Gary, the son of an English immigrant; Elijah, the high school dropout and Gary, the multi-degreed Jesuit priest. The two of us had long been locked into a mutual appreciation and admiration, and we respected each other's opinion. I told him that nothing could be done now—or down the line—if he didn't have an arm. He agreed, but, damn, he still wanted to do some damage to his girlfriend.

I persuaded him that he was better off being cool about things and to allow me to take him to the hospital.

We went to the hospital and finessed our way around the the intake nurse who looked at us suspiciously, under her raised eybrows, when I lied about a kitchen accident. The police were not called. After the repairs had been done, Elijah and I talked about a strategy for anger control. He settled down, hugged me with his good arm, and took off. He'll be okay.

Thursday, May 9th

Kay, my steady staff person, has struggled a lot over Rob, an articulate, piercing-eyes Nam Vet. He is dying of AIDS. The temptation for the drug addict with AIDS is simply to overdose him or herself and put an end to the misery. And he has been in misery. He is a forthright person who has taken Kay into that realm of honesty and disclosure which few can imagine. It is tough on her; she loves Rob very much.

If each one of my staff over the years had written a journal recounting his or her experiences, they would have dealt with—at some point—the emotional highs and lows of walking with a particular street person. It would be a journal of a staff person who has been turned to for sharing, solace, counsel, laughter, tears, rebuke, anger, cajoling, a hug, ball scores, money, a theological discussion, food, prayer, tips on romance, intervention with friends and enemies, comfort, political opinions, assistance in dying, and advice on virtually anything the human mind can dream up. Like Kay with Rob, each staff person has known the sleepless nights and the endless racking of one's brain for possible solutions to a complex problem. He or she has felt the helplessness that comes in the face of things out of their control, the excitment of unsolicited love received and given, the emptiness of a known guest who has disappeared, the joy of a new baby, and the frustration of a senseless death. Every staff person could write about that reamed-out, ground-out, wiped-out feeling at the end of the week and yet, just as quickly, point to the exhilaration of being party to some small or great achievement by one of our guests in education or employment. And, I think, if that hypothetical journal were written, there would be not a few entries about sacred moments when prayers were whispered for a particular individual known and loved.

In the end, Kay will give her heart to Rob. She knows that dramatic changes in addiction or in sickness are unlikely. At the same time, it is clear that she is in this guy's life for the long haul. She has an unconditional love. This is what he—or any of our guests—will judge to be the most important gift that can be given.

Friday, May 10th

Kevin, one of the staff, was reflecting on a guest who seems to be a born peace-maker. He wrote this in a recent newsletter:

Street life is violent. It takes courage to stand against this fact, to lower the walls erected to protect self, in order to show a side which cries for peace. I am continually awed by those of our guests who choose this harder, less popular path. These prophets, facing harsh realities which force many to think and act only in terms of preserving themselves, call instead for a radical state: namely, an atmosphere in which sisters and brothers cooperate and solve conflicts constructively and reject violence as an acceptable option. They claim with Reverend King for all on the streets to hear: "Either we learn to live together as brothers, or we will perish together as fools."

Wednesday, May 23rd

Holding his pants up, wearing one sock, one shoe, and a torn shirt, Andy stood before me after breakfast. In some ways, he follows the pattern of many of the mentally ill on the streets: dysfunction, hospitalization, medication, stability, discharge, gradual deterioration, dysfunction, and back to hospitalization. In spite of his mental illness, Andy is in touch with the natural world around him. And it is a touch of compassion.

This morning, he sought my help in rescuing some birds. Some people were throwing bread crumbs into the middle of the street, and he feared that the sparrows would be run over by indiscriminating motorists. He asked if I could please ask people not to throw food out in the street? Yes, I could. I went outside, thinking it was better to let Andy have some peace, rather than get into an explanation of how fast and car-savvy these inner city sparrows can be. Another time, Andy came to me in search of a claw hammer. He told me of a nearby emaciated tree that was in pain because a nail had been driven into it. He removed the nail. No surgeon ever operated with such skill and care on a patient.

Saturday, June 1st

Now that the word is getting out that I am leaving Nativity House and planning on going to a language school in Bolivia, our guests have been offering all kinds of suggestions for my time away. The dreams of people and their love for me come in a wonderful mix.

"When you go to Bulgaria, get lots of skiing in."

"Come on down to Oregon, and camp out by the river with me and some of my friends."

"When you get to Australia, eat lots of bananas and put on some weight."

"Have the Pope pull your pink slip, get yourself a good woman, rent a motel room for two weeks, and go to it. Be sure there is air conditioning."

"Could you visit my son in the New Jersey State Penitentiary? He wants to be a priest."

"Maybe you could score on some good Columbian dope, sell it back here, and it would give us enough money to build another bathroom in Nativity House."

"I hear Panama is not as cold as Tacoma, but if you need an extra jacket I can get you one."

"Don't talk to strangers, and don't hitchhike. There are a lot of weirdos out there."

"Take lots of good books, especially a good Bible. I have an extra one if you need it. And take lots of toilet paper."

"Find some peace away from this madness, Father, and find as good a friend as you have been to us."

Sunday, June 9th

There is an evil quality about this man, Clark. I can smell it, feel it, taste it. He is always pushing me to the limit in a subtle and clever way, threatening without proving his point. He is full of hatred, but it is focused, directed, manipulative. Today at Mass I kicked him out, for nonstop talking. I publically redressed him for disturbing all the brothers and sisters who were there to pray. It was a heart-thumping confrontation, even though I was surrounded by a host of good and supportive people. As he was slowly—defiantly—heading for the door, I felt his power; his disdain for me reached through the crowded room, grabbing me like a hand around my throat.

It is a tough one to sort out, tonight. I feel like I am meeting something much bigger, much more sinister, than Clark alone. I name it "evil." Whatever it is, I know it to be seductive, powerful, and seeking annihilation. Is it so entrenched that I'll never be able to reach this guy, that no one—not even the most holy, most wise, and the most hip—will be able to touch his heart?

Yet I believe God can reach him, and God can turn that seeming heart of stone into a heart of flesh. I pray for Clark tonight and for the calming of my fear and agitation.

Friday, June 28th

Alton dropped his well-traveled duffle bag on the floor and took me into his arms. He is a great big guy—of body and of spirit. It was time to leave this morning, heading by Greyhound to New Orleans to join his family and begin work. He has always been a worker, even when he got strung out on drugs. Now "the past is past," as he would say, and he looked foward to a productive and drug-free life.

He pulled out forty bucks and gave it to me.

I said, "No, no way."

He said, "Yes."

It was his way of saying thanks for our help, and it was clear, looking into his eyes, that his need to give was much greater than my silly protestations. This was the widow's mite. He had just about enough for hamburgers and coke and a candy bar in the three-day trip, and Nativity House was getting a portion of it.

And Jesus said, "She from the little she had
　　has put in all she had to live on." (Lk. 21:4)

Have a safe trip, Alton. When I leave Tacoma, may I leave with such dignity.

Saturday, July 6th

Tyrone and Blue surprised me today, two old veterans from my first year here. They have been off the streets for years, coinciding with when they gave up drinking. They had heard that I was leaving and came in to pay their respects. Blue, a playful, quick-witted man, handsome, and gray-haired, had lost his voice box to cancer a few years back, and so carried on his conversation with one of those voice-augmentation gadgets that he placed on his throat, which gave his voice an artificial sound. But it did not diminish his smile and humor. Tyrone, reflective, a Shakespeare lover, reminded me gratefully of when I had literally carried him into the hospital nearly dead in his tracks from booze-induced malnutrition.

It was a gentle moment between old friends.

Sunday, July 7th

What a captivating scene it was somewhere in this busy day. Willie, a tall and lanky vagabond, whipped out his harmonica and played a Blues rendition of some obscure melody. And Bernice, a sixty-year-old woman who lives in a nearby group residence, listened intently, grinning from ear to ear, knowing that the music was strictly for her pleasure. In all her life, she had never had, I'm sure, her own private concert. Whatever suffering and grief these two had known in life—these two mutual strangers—it was dispelled for a moment by the red-hot, get-down harmonica playing of a red-hot, get-down Willie.

Sunday, July 14th

I have seen the death that is the result of street violence: people stabbed, shot, strangled, stomped. I have identified people in the morgue, watched paramedics carry away dead or dying from sidewalks, motley hotel rooms, bars, and shelters. In the seven years I have been here, no one has ever been killed in Nativity House.

Today we came close. Mason, a paranoid schizophrenic, in and out of the hospital, was convinced that there was a conspiracy against him, and and that it was being orchestrated by both the CIA and a collection of undercover space aliens. He lost it this morning with Leslie, an out-of-work accountant from California and a totally innocent bystander, who had made a harmless comment about the broken string on Mason's guitar. As Leslie turned away, Mason removed a knife from the guitar case and put it into Leslie's back. Two quick thrusts.

Blood was pouring on to the floor. Leslie staggered to a couch. Mason turned to me as I ran to the scene, handed me the knife, placed his hands on the wall in a spread-eagle fashion and waited for me to make an arrest. It was bizarre and scary. In the meantime, staff had called 911, and the police and paramedics arrived on the scene quickly.

Leslie is going to be okay, although his kidney was nicked, and he lost a lot of blood. When I saw him at the hospital, he assured me that he was all right. It was a close call. Tonight, I feel like the pilot who flew safely through a hurricane, wondering if he will survive another storm tomorrow.

Tuesday, July 16th

Less than two weeks now. I am like a man trying to hold back a tidal wave of memories and people. It is impossible. I have joyfully resigned myself to let it happen as it will happen. The larger part of me wants to be present to every moment and every encounter. Neil, Kay, Pam, and Kevin are very present to me, not knowing exactly how to ease the events of the countdown, yet ever solicitous of my feelings. Every day now, at our end-of-the-day evaluation, the focus is on me. The roles have been reversed, and the point man is being led by the very people he has led; it is a combination of the protection and challenge that all teachers must have with their fragile students.

I have always told my staff, especially those who are about to leave permanently, that they need to go to the end and not psychologically check out prematurely. They should embrace even the last minutes here on the streets, believing that God's Providence may be preparing them for the concluding moments. Everything: guests (dead or alive), conversations, confrontations, frustrations, insights, tears, laughs, successes, failures. It may all come down to the final day, the final moment, the final person.

Saturday, July 20th

There has been a lot of not-so-secret card signing going on. I have been receiving them day after day. They are the signs of goodbye and the signs of love. The guests of Nativity House cannot give me enough gifts.

I have been given poems, coffee mugs, baseball caps, a rosary, candy bars, T-shirts, a wooden carving, framed quotations, a pocket knife, an Eric Clapton album, a tiny Bible, a West African cap, some homemade chocolate chippers, a lunch at Dairy Bell ("give him a double order of fries"), a pair of sweat socks, a six-pack of Pepsi, photographs of families, silver crosses on chains, and a giant drawing of a giraffe done in crayola.

Most of the folks leave me with hugs and handshakes and that tender look which only attends deep emotion.

Sunday, July 28th

It was the last Mass I would do at Nativity House. As I was beginning, I thought of a fragment from Raymond Carver's poem, "Proposal." He was reflecting on his imminent death and the importance of sharing his feelings with the woman he loved:

. . . . This/ was it, so any holding back had to
be stupid, had to be/ insane and meager.
How many ever get to this? I thought/
at the time. It's not far from here to needing/
a celebration, a joining, a bringing of friends
into it,/ a handing out of champagne and/ Perrier.

I told my congregation that I was grateful to have been able to pray with them. They had taught me of God, and of what Nativity House could be, and had helped me to be a better person.

In the middle of my homily, Charles started snoring. He was so loud that we had to wake him up. Later on, someone got stuck in the bathroom and kept flushing the toilet. At communion time, Kathy came up early and, while waiting for me to finish my prayers, she chatted with two of her inner voices. She was giving them the lowdown on me.

It may have been a unique moment, and it may have been the end of an era, and some things may not have gone smoothly, but it was a joyful final Mass at Nativity House.

Saturday, August 3rd

Sitting at home, gazing out the window. This final day has been a whirlwind. Lots of goodbyes. Overwhelmed. Captured.

A dear friend and a former teacher of mine, who is a Baptist Minister, once told me about his ordination to the ministry. During the ceremony, his congregation expressed the truth that the dignity and responsibilities of the priesthood came from the people and were for the people. They did this through the sacred gesture of placing their hands upon his head.

I thought of that image today as our guests were saying goodbye to me. They embraced me, placing their hearts upon my heart.

Bibliography

Bernanos, Georges, *Diary of a Country Priest*. New York: The Macmillan Company, 1969.

Carver, Raymond, *A New Path to the Waterfall*. New York: Atlantic Monthly Press, 1990.

Hopkins, Gerard Manley, *Gerard Manley Hopkins*. London: Penguin Classics, 1953.

Jerusalem Bible. Garden City, New York: Doubleday & Company, Garden City, 1966.

LeFerve, Perry D. (ed.), *The Prayers of Soren Kierkegaard*. Chicago: University of Chicago Press, 1963.

Miller, Arthur, *After the Fall*. New York: Viking Press, New York, 1964.

Moody, John, *John Henry Newman*. New York: Sheed & Ward, 1945.